WARNE'S
Complete Letter Writer

Compiled by
Wendy and Tom Hartman

FREDERICK WARNE

Published by Frederick Warne (Publishers) Ltd, London

Revised edition 1983
© 1983 by Frederick Warne (Publishers) Ltd
Reprinted 1984

Case bound edition ISBN 0 7232 2989 9
Paper back edition ISBN 0 7232 2998 8

Printed in Great Britain
by Butler & Tanner Ltd,
Frome and London
D 7202.1183

Contents

Acknowledgements

The editors would particularly like to thank the following for their advice and assistance in the compilation of this book: Harold Corker of the National Westminster Bank Ltd; Mr and Mrs Paul Daffarn; Colin Shaw of Wilkins Kennedy & Co; John Mitchell; also Mrs Cleonie Stenhouse of the Lumley Employment Agency and D. B. Wallace of United Cargo Containers Ltd.

Preface

This book is a practical guide to letter writing in business and private life. The letters themselves should *not be copied word for word*, but their general style should be followed, so that the reader will learn the difference in tone, for example, between a business letter and a letter to an acquaintance or friend, and will learn how to write a balanced, well-expressed letter, how to begin and end it correctly, and how to address the envelope correctly.

The book is divided into two parts. The first half of Part One has an introductory section on the handling of business correspondence, and on how to set out a business letter, followed by specimen letters. These letters are such as the ordinary man engaged in business would use to deal with matters that are likely to arise. Letters concerning employment are also included in this section. The second half of Part One is concerned with letters of a social nature that might occur in connection with business.

Part Two contains specimen letters concerning domestic and social matters: invitations, announcements, congratulations, etc. Others deal with education, careers, holidays, house purchase, insurance, and a hundred and one other things which members of a family might require.

Introduction to Letter Writing

Beginning a Letter – Ending a Letter – The Envelope

There are certain accepted ways of beginning and ending a letter, of setting it out and of addressing the envelope, the more usual of which are given here.

Beginning a Letter

It is customary to put the address of the writer at the top right-hand corner of the first page of the letter. If the house has a name as well as a number, this is written above the number. The postcode should appear below the name of the town or city. This consists of two unpunctuated groups, usually of three letters or figures each, but varies in different parts of the country. The date should always be included just below the address, eg:

MAYFIELD,
4 MEWS WAY,
HATFIELD.
(postcode)
1st June 19--

Telephone: Hatfield 000

Dear Mr Brown,
      etc.

If printed or engraved writing paper is used, the address and telephone number are often placed in the centre, near the top of the page. The date may then be placed on the right-hand side of the page, a little lower than the address, or centred under the address.

It is important to include the full date in any letter, whether it is a business letter or one to a friend. It should be written as follows: 15th March 19--.

In letters of an official or business nature the name and address of the person to whom one is writing should be placed just above the *Dear Sir*, on the left-hand side of the letter, or, rather less formally, at the bottom left-hand corner of the letter, to the left of the signature:

8 THE MOUNT,
CAMBRIDGE.
(postcode)
3rd March 19--

The Headmistress,
St Catherine's School,
Bexhill-on-Sea,
Sussex.

Dear Madam,

Forms of Address for Opening a Letter*

Dear Sir, Dear Madam is the usual form in business letters, or in letters to strangers. *Dear Madam* includes both married and single women; Dear Miss, on its own, is never used. *Sir, Madam* is more formal than *Dear Sir*; *Dear Madam,* is usually employed only with a particularly formal letter and should be used with care as it sometimes denotes displeasure on the part of the writer. Never use the phrase *Dear Sir/or Madam*; if the sex of the person to whom one is writing is unknown, *Dear Sir,* irrespective of sex, is the correct form, except for a circular business letter.

In writing to acquaintances the surname and title are used: *Dear Mr Smith, Dear Mrs Smith, Dear Miss Smith*. The ugly neologism *Dear Ms Smith* should be avoided. It cannot be pronounced and is not an abbreviation of anything.

For close friends the Christian name will be used: *Dear John*. It is usually safe to use the Christian name if it would normally be used by the writer in conversation. In the past it was common for men friends to address each other by their surnames, but this is now considered rather condescending.

In correspondence with strangers it is usual to change from *Dear Sir* to *Dear Mr* —— after one or two letters have been exchanged. In writing a social letter to a stranger of one's own age and position the name and title are generally used (if known) in preference to *Dear Sir*.

The prefix *My* in front of *dear* is used in Great Britain only in front of

*See also Appendix I (p 201)

a Christian name and among friends. In America, however, *My dear Miss Smith* is more formal than *Dear Miss Smith*; the two countries use the word *My* in opposite ways to indicate the degree of cordiality between the correspondents.

Ending a Letter*

Yours faithfully is the correct ending for all business letters or letters of a non-social nature which have begun with *Dear Sir* or *Dear Madam*. A letter can be made more formal by the addition of *I am* or *I remain*:

I am (*or* I remain)

Yours faithfully,

JOHN SMITH

Yours truly is used as an alternative to *Yours faithfully* when one does not know the recipient.

Yours sincerely should be used to end a business letter which has started with the name of the recipient: *Dear Mr Jones. With best wishes* or *With kind regards* may be added to business letters if the correspondents know each other.

Your obedient servant is never used now in general correspondence except to people of certain ranks on formal occasions and by certain Government departments. All that is necessary in most cases, in business letters, (including letters making application for jobs) is *Yours faithfully*, and in social letters *Yours sincerely*.

A more intimate greeting than *Yours sincerely* is *Yours ever. Yours* is sometimes used between men friends and between men and women, and *With love from* between girl friends and members of one's family. Such letters are generally signed with the Christian name only:

Yours ever,

JOHN

The Signature: Women should indicate their title after their signature if this is necessary, as it usually is in business letters:

Margaret Smith (Miss)

Margaret Smith (Mrs)

*See also Appendix I (p 201)

11

The Envelope*

Men's names are written thus:

> *Henry Smith, Esq.,* or
> *Mr H. Smith*

Distinctions follow the name:

> *Henry Smith, Esq., BA*

Married Women usually take their husband's initials:

> *Mrs H. Smith*

Widows retain their late husband's initial. In the case of *divorcees*, they are usually addressed by their own initial or Christian name:

> *Mrs Diana Smith*

Single Women are addressed thus:

> *Miss Margaret Smith*

A *firm* takes the collective title of *Messrs* if there are two or more people in the name, and if its *not* a limited company:

> *Messrs Brown & Jones*

If it *is* a limited company, *Messrs* is not used:

> *Smith & Co. Ltd*

A firm such as *All Light Electric Co. Ltd* does not, of course, need to be preceded by Messrs.

*See also Appendix I (p 201)

PART ONE:

The Business Letter Writer

Business Correspondence

Its Importance
General Considerations
The Layout of a Business Letter
Style
Correspondence References
Dealing with Correspondence
The Postman
Telex

Model Letters

Letters between Employers and Employees

13

Letters of Application for Employment

Letters to and from Sales Representatives

Letters about Finance

Tradesmen's Letters

Business Correspondence

Its Importance

It is essential that any man or woman employed in business is able to write a clear, suitable letter that fulfils exactly the object for which it is written and leaves a favourable impression on the recipient. Business cannot be conducted without letters, for even though the telephone or telex may initiate most matters of business, a letter confirming the matter in hand is almost invariably necessary. Unsuitable letters hinder business and cause confusion and loss, while well-conducted correspondence is a sign of the efficiency that is so strong a factor in success.

General Considerations

The choice of stationery should be carefully made. Letter paper should always be good, but not too thick or expensive looking, which gives an impression of waste and pretentiousness. The heading should be printed, and it is is a mistake to get this done too cheaply. A good, plain, appropriate heading, which gives your correspondents all the information about yourself that is needed, and perhaps some useful information about your business, is a good investment. The task of designing it is not easy. Let a good graphic artist, who specializes in this kind of work, do it for you.

A good heading is always a good advertisement, but it is a bad, although common, practice to make it *look* like an advertisement. Never disfigure your stationery by blatant assertions about yourself or your business which will make your correspondents regard you as being on the level of a market-square cheap-jack. A tradesman or businessman may use a bolder heading than a banker or a solicitor, but there is no reason why it should not be just as dignified.

Every heading should contain: the full style of the firm, the full postal address, telephone number, telex number and a short description of the firm, such as *Wholesale Ironmongers, Art and Commercial Printers, etc*. A heading may also contain such information as the names of the partners, the addresses of branch offices, the date of the establishment of the firm (if it is an old one), and a list of any notable specialities in which the firm deals. An illustration of the firm's works is sometimes given but, if this is done, it should be small, neat and attractively worked into the scheme of the heading.

The Layout of a Business Letter

A letter should always be typed or written to have the appearance of 'fitting' the paper. It should never be squeezed up at the top or begun low down on the sheet, with the end crowded in at the bottom.

If a printed heading is used, the date will be placed beneath it on the right-hand side of the paper. Nearly level with it on the left-hand side should be placed your reference number, and below this the name and address of your correspondent:

Ref. XL/48   18th April 19--

Fuller & White P.L.C.,
18 Cheapside, EC2.

Dear Sirs,

Then will follow the body of the letter. This should be so arranged as to leave the same amount of space at the bottom of the formal conclusion and signature as appears at the top between the printed heading and the body of the letter. This of course can be varied according to the length of the letter.

The formal conclusion and signature are always placed towards the right-hand side, thus:

Yours faithfully,

B. S. Manton

The writer must *always* sign the letter by hand. If the signature is not legible, or the surname unusual, the name may be typed underneath. The signature should always be the same. Don't vary it by signing one letter *John Smith* and the next *J. T. Smith*. Fanciful and ornate signatures should be avoided. They are seldom legible, look pretentious and do not create a good impression in business.

When signing on behalf of a firm or a third party, the name of the firm and the writer should be typed, and the writer must also sign the letter, thus:

Yours faithfully

For Fuller & White P.L.C.,

(signature)

F. Smith

The width of the margins is a matter of taste, but they should be uniform. Wide margins give a much better appearance than narrow ones and certainly have the advantage of making a letter easy to read. The eye is soon tired by too long a line. A margin of $2\frac{1}{2}$cm on each side is usually considered sufficient.

A letter should never be typed or written so as to present a solid block of matter which your correspondent feels disinclined to read. A long letter must be broken up into separate paragraphs. It is not always wise to follow the rule that a paragraph should be given to each subject. Different aspects of the same subject may be given separate paragraphs, and each paragraph should rarely exceed six or eight lines. It is also a good plan to tabulate your letter whenever possible. This makes it clear, concise, adequate, and gives the impression of courtesy and consideration, instead of hurry and abruptness.

Style

Business letters must not be written in a jargon consisting of words and phrases which one would not think of using in everyday life. Most of the stereotyped phrases which constitute the stock-in-trade of some business correspondents can be dispensed with. Plain English is much better.

Two points are all-important – clarity and conciseness. Be sure to say precisely what you mean and say it in as few words as possible. Do not add a lot of unnecessary information.

On the other hand, do not be abrupt, and take care to avoid giving your correspondent the impression that you haven't the time, or do not think him of sufficient importance, to take trouble over your letter to him. For the same reason the excessive use of contractions (eg don't, haven't) should be avoided. They have the appearance of saving yourself trouble at your correspondent's expense. Always sit down to write a letter with the aim of pleasing the recipient.

A would-be smart correspondent might think the following letter a good specimen:

Dear Sirs,

Yr favour of the 11th inst. to hand, and same has our best attentn. We beg to state, however, that price quoted was rock-bottom, and no disct. from this can be given. Our invoices for this class of goods are rendered strictly net – please note for future guidance.

Assuring you that your favours shall always have our best attentn.,

We beg to remain
Yrs. faithfully,

In fact, it could hardly be worse. The contractions scattered about it save very little time, and their use is discourteous to the recipient. The point of the letter – that a discount cannot be allowed – is stated with unnecessary brusqueness. The writer then adds a complimentary sentence, which, after the curtness of the preceding note, is bound to appear insincere. Worst of all, the letter is not in plain English. 'Favour', 'to hand', 'same', 'we beg to state', 'rock-bottom' are all hackneyed phrases which are merely disfigurements.

Compare it with a similar letter written in simple English:

Dear Sirs,

We acknowledge receipt of your letter of 11th January. We regret, however, that we are not able to allow any discount from the price quoted, and our invoices for this class of goods are rendered strictly net. We shall be obliged if you will make a note of this for your guidance in future transactions.

Yours faithfully,

Correspondence References

The purpose of references is to speed location of previous correspondence in the files and identify which department or individual was responsible for it. To those ends the system used should be as clear and simple as possible. In a small office the date alone may be sufficient. In a company of any size the initials of the person or department sending the letter, and possibly those of the typist, should form part of the reference. This is particularly helpful if the reply is by telephone and the signature is illegible or a name not given.

Identification may be more speedy if the first letters of the subject are used, in conjunction with numbers if the subject is subdivided. For example, a wholesaler in tools might use GAR as a prefix for gardening tools, with a number referring to a type of tool. Such a reference might read 'GAR22/jm.rth', using capitals only for the subject reference. The reply can then be related to the department and the individual concerned even by someone, perhaps only temporary, who has not mastered a full numerical system.

Replies to correspondence should always quote any reference given. Many company letter headings make provision for this. If not, the reference can logically be placed beneath the address to which the reply is being sent, or used as part of the heading to the letter:

Complete Tool Wholesales Ltd,
Woodside,
Mitcham, Surrey.
Your ref: GAR22/jm.rth

Our ref: -----

Dear Sirs,
Thank you for your letter of 3rd March . . .

Or:

Dear Sirs,

Supply of hand forks, your ref: GAR22/jm.rth

Thank you for your letter of 3rd March ...

Dealing with Correspondence

The first essential in dealing quickly and effectively with correspondence is the adoption of a suitable system of filing. The systems of filing offered for the businessman's consideration today are numerous, but they nearly all come under two headings – filing by the names of the correspondents, or by subjects. If in doubt, a good commercial stationer will help you to decide on the best system for your own particular needs.

For businesses in which the correspondence is not very large there is little doubt that the best plan is to file the letters received, with carbon duplicates of the letters written in reply, in chronological order, so that a complete history of the transactions is available. The complete correspondence is then filed either under the initial letter of the correspondent's name, or under subject matter, with a cross-reference to the name.

Incoming letters should be stamped with the date of receipt and marked off to the person or department that is to deal with them.

Letters should, properly, deal with only one subject, otherwise the reference system will be defeated or become so complex as to be difficult to operate.

The Postman

The majority of firms, unless very small, use franking machines in preference to postage stamps. They speed the work and avoid the hazard of quite large sums being held in the form of stamps. The 'postman' needs to take care in applying the correct postage. Additionally he will be responsible for making out recorded delivery and registered letter forms and keeping the counterfoils. A small 'float' of stamps is nearly always necessary for mail going out after the general office has closed. If a stamp book is kept, there should also be a simple account of the money as in a petty cash book.

Telex

A particular advantage of the telex is that both sender and recipient have a typewritten copy of the message, which avoids misunderstandings arising from conversation, but has the benefit of speed. For the sake of economy telex messages are usually concise and brief, unless detailed information is essential. Companies not having their own telex machines can use telex bureaux.

MODEL LETTERS

Letters Between Employers and Employees

1   From an Employee, Asking for Promotion

14 ANGEL CLARE CLOSE,
DORCHESTER.
(postcode)
14th October 19--

F. Derriman Esq.,
Managing Director,
Derriman & Co. Ltd,
Industrial Estate,
Dorchester.

Dear Mr Derriman,

I have just heard that Mr Loveday is to retire at the end of the year and am very sad to learn that ill-health has forced this decision upon him. He will be much missed both as a friend and a colleague.

May I ask you, when you come to consider replacing him, to bear me in mind? I have, as you know, been on the road for twelve years now and, much as I have enjoyed my work, I feel that it is time for me to move to an 'in-house' job. I think I can say that I have given Bob Loveday satisfaction and, knowing what I do of his work, I am confident that I could fill his place to your satisfaction.

Yours sincerely,
THOMAS HUNT

24

2   From an Employee, Excusing his Absence Owing to Sickness

CASTLE DERRY,
TORPOINT,
CORNWALL.
(postcode)
4th January 19--

J. M. Penrose Esq.,
Tamar Trading P.L.C.,
Torpoint,
Cornwall.

Dear Mr Penrose,

Further to my wife's telephone call yesterday, I have now seen my doctor who says that I have a slight attack of bronchitis and should stay at home for the rest of the week. I enclose a certificate and ask you to accept my apologies for any inconvenience my absence may cause.

Yours sincerely,

B. K. INGLIS

3   From an Employee, Excusing his Absence on Compassionate Grounds

107 FOUNTAIN SQUARE,
CARLISLE.
(postcode)
18th September 19--

J. R. Dodd Esq.,
Brown and Dodd Ltd,
58 County Square,
London SW1.

Dear Mr Dodd,

I regret to say that I shall be away from the office all next week. My brother died suddenly in Carlisle on Friday; I received the news just in time to catch the overnight train. My sister-in-law is very shocked and I'm afraid that I shall have to stay here and make arrangements for the funeral. I do apologize for any inconvenience that my absence may cause but I'm sure you will understand.

Yours sincerely,

WILLIAM THOMPSON

4 From an Employee, Giving Formal Notice

91 HORSE LANE,
HASLEMERE.
(postcode)
1st July 19--

J. B. Driscoll Esq.,
Sibert & Nephew P.L.C.,
19 Scott Road,
Guildford,
Surrey.

Dear Mr Driscoll,

It is with sincere regret that I write to tell you that, after much reflection, I have accepted the job of Sales Manager at Cather & Cather, which was offered to me some weeks ago. It is no exaggeration to say that I have enjoyed every day of my work at Sibert's and the great kindness you have shown me is something which I shall recall with the deepest gratitude, but I am sure you will appreciate that, at this stage in my career, it is an opportunity which I could scarcely let slip. Cathers would like me to start work on 1st November when the statutory period of my notice has elapsed, but if you can possibly spare me a week or two earlier I should be grateful.

Once again may I say how sorry I am to be leaving and how much I appreciate all that you have done for me.

Yours very sincerely,
OSWALD HENSHAWE

5 From an Employee Asking for a Reference

Private and Confidential

191 LONGFORD LANE,
LONDON SW9.
29th September 19--

The Manager,
Joseph Mist and Sons,
159 Riverton Road,
London SW11.

Dear Sir,

I should like to apply for a post in the Civil Service, which I have seen advertised and, as I have to send three references with my application, I should be very much obliged if you would give me a letter of recommendation. You will see from the advertisement, which I enclose, the kind of work which is entailed.

I make so bold as to believe that you have always been satisfied with my work, and I hope you will say all you can in my favour. The post is a very good one and seems to offer good prospects of advancement.

If my application is not successful, I trust you will not think that I am dissatisfied with my position here. I am applying for this post only because I feel it would give me a better position and salary.

Yours faithfully,
J. W. Obwangor

6   A General Reference

To Whom it May Concern

Mr Obwangor has worked for this company for the past five years, during which time he has proved himself to be a man of integrity, reliability, intelligence and initiative. He is very popular with his colleagues, but is obliged to leave us for unavoidable personal reasons. We shall all be very sorry to lose him.

G. L. Onama
3rd October 19--

7   Taking up a Reference

[Business Address]
5th October 19--

Private and Confidential

The Personnel Manager,
Harding & Hicks P.L.C.,
Battersea Broadway.

Dear Sir,

Mr John Marlowe informs me that he was employed by you for four years as a salesman in your photographic department. He has applied for a job as a salesman in our Ilford branch and has given the name of your company as a reference. I should be much obliged if you could tell me whether you found him honest and reliable, whether he knows his subject and why he left your employ. Needless to say your answer will be treated in the strictest confidence.

Yours faithfully,

S. MANDERSON
Director
Trent Photographic Ltd

8   A Favourable Reference

[BUSINESS ADDRESS]
9th October 19--

Private and Confidential

S. Manderson Esq.,
Director,
Trent Photographic Ltd.

Dear Mr Manderson,

In answer to your letter about John Marlowe, I am glad to hear that he is able to consider taking a job once again. For personal reasons he was obliged to leave us to go and live with his family in Ilford; we were very sorry to lose him. He is a thoroughly honest and reliable young man and has an excellent knowledge of photography. He is tidy, friendly and well-mannered, and will, I am sure, give you every satisfaction. Please give him my kind regards.

Yours sincerely,
ROBERT BENTLEY

9   A Qualified Reference

[BUSINESS ADDRESS]
9th October 19--

Private and Confidential

S. Manderson Esq.,
Director,
Trent Photographic Ltd.

Dear Mr Manderson,

In answer to your letter making inquiries about Mr John Marlowe, I can assure you that he is a scrupulously honest, intelligent and well-mannered young man who has a sound grasp of all aspects of photography. Unfortunately his domestic problems steadily encroached upon his work, until, out of fairness to other members of the staff, I had to ask him to leave. I was, nevertheless, sorry to lose him. If he has now managed to sort out his private life, I'm sure that you will find him an excellent employee.

Yours sincerely,
ROBERT BENTLEY

10   Refusing a Reference

[BUSINESS ADDRESS]
9th October 19--

Private and Confidential

S. Manderson Esq.,
Director,
Trent Photographic Ltd.
Dear Mr Manderson,

In reply to your letter making inquiries about Mr John Marlowe, I told him when he left us that I would not be prepared to give him a reference and the passage of time has done nothing to alter that decision. Under the circumstances I would rather say no more.

Yours sincerely,
ROBERT BENTLEY

11   Engaging a Clerk

[BUSINESS ADDRESS]
30th March 19--

T. V. Bell Esq.,
78a Southwold Parade,
Portsmouth,
Hampshire.
Dear Mr Bell,

I have now taken up your references and, as they are quite satisfactory, I should be glad if you would start work here as arranged on Monday next at 9.30 a.m. Please ask for Mr Mortimer, who is expecting you.

As agreed at the interview, your salary will be £--- a year, plus Luncheon Vouchers at the rate of 45p per day. The hours of work are from 9.30 a.m. to 5.30 p.m. with four weeks holiday each year. After a trial period of one month, assuming you prove to be satisfactory, you will be given a Contract of Employment. After serving for one year, you will be eligible to join the Company's Contributory Pension Scheme.

I look forward to seeing you on the 5th April.

Yours sincerely,

S. S. JONES
Personnel Director

12   Making an Employee Redundant

[BUSINESS ADDRESS]
17th August 19--

Dear Mr Pearce,

I am sorry to inform you that, owing to the severe recession, the company is having to reduce its workforce by one-third. The work of the particular kind in which you were involved has greatly diminished.

As you have completed more than two years with the company, you will be eligible for redundancy pay according to the scales laid down in the Redundancy Payments Act, 1965.

Yours sincerely,
For H. R. Ball & Sons

P. WHITE
Director

13   Dismissing an Employee

[BUSINESS ADDRESS]
17th August 19--

Dear Mr Spark,

Following the final written warning dated . . . . , there has been no improvement in your behaviour and therefore, on behalf of the firm, I have to inform you that your services will not be required by the company after the end of this month. If you so wish, you may leave immediately and your wages will be made up to the end of the month.

Yours faithfully
For the Eezi-ars Chair Co.

C. T. JONES
Partner

14 Warning Letter Under the Employment Protection Act

[BUSINESS ADDRESS]
10th October 19--

Dear Mr Copeman,

Would you please accept this letter as a formal warning under the Employment Protection Act 1975. Your behaviour towards clients of the firm and other staff members is causing great embarrassment, and unless the situation improves within the next month, the partners will have no alternative but to issue a final written warning, following which any recurrence will lead to suspension or even dismissal.

Yours faithfully,

J. MORRIS

Letters of Application for Employment

In applying for jobs the applicant should always state age and experience, if any. If qualifications are long, it is often better to write a short covering note and to attach a typewritten note of qualifications to the covering letter. Also, the reason for applying should be given, and any details (such as hobbies) which help the prospective employer to judge the applicant's personality. Letters should be brief and to the point, and should be clearly written or typed.

Applicants should always state their ability to provide references.

15 Applying for a Job as a Telephone Engineer

20 CLOVER GARDENS,
LONDON SW7.
12th December 19--

The Post Office

Dear Sirs,

I am seeking a job as Telephone Engineer and should be glad to know whether you have any vacancies. I have passed the TEC Certificate and

I am taking classes for the National Certificate. I am 18 years of age.

Yours faithfully,

DANIEL REED

16 Applying for a Job as a Monotype Operator

144 WINDLESHAM DRIVE,
LIVERPOOL.
(postcode)
12th October 19--

Box No. 127,
Caxton Magazine.

Dear Sirs,

I am interested in your advertisement in the 'Caxton Magazine' for a keyboard operator. I am 29 years of age, married, and my typesetting experience is as follows:

After leaving Hixley Comprehensive School (with four 'O' Levels and one 'A' Level), I was apprenticed to the Southern Press in London. During my apprenticeship I attended the London School of Printing and gained their Diploma for Monotype Composition (hot-metal) in 1970. In 1975 I joined J. Roberts P.L.C. in Liverpool, a company which specializes in bookwork. While here I have re-trained onto Monophoto equipment and more recently to the Linotron 202 system.

I believe that my qualifications match those for which you are looking, and that my present employers are satisfied with my work.

For personal reasons I am now seeking work in the London area and greatly hope that my application will be successful.

Yours faithfully,

JOHN DODD

17 Applying for a Job as a Shorthand Typist

153 LONDON WAY,
GOLDSTONE,
SURREY.
(postcode)
2nd January 19--

Box No. 153,
The Daily Telegraph.

Dears Sirs,

Your advertisement in today's 'Daily Telegraph' for a senior shorthand typist interests me greatly.

I am twenty years of age and achieved four 'O' Levels before leaving school at the age of sixteen. I then attended my local college of further education where I qualified in shorthand (110 words per minute) and typing (60 words per minute). The course also included general secretarial training.

My present employer has increased my responsibilities in the three years that I have worked for his Company. My work includes operating the telex machine and I have had some experience in using a simple word-processor. During the past year I have been dealing with most of the general correspondence on my own initiative, and presenting my replies for the Manager's signature. My present salary is £---.

I am anxious to extend my experience and should much appreciate the opportunity of an interview.

I look forward to hearing from you.

Yours faithfully
SUSIE BELLGEON

18   Applying for a Job as a Private Secretary

112 MERTON MANOR ROAD,
CROFTWOOD,
ESSEX.
(postcode)
5th June 19--

Dear Sir,

I have heard from a friend that you are seeking a reliable private secretary and I wonder whether you would be willing to grant me an interview.

I was educated at Merton College for Girls, where I took GCE 'O' Level and passed in English, French, History and Geography. I am now 25 and for the past five years have been Private Secretary to the Managing Director of Smith & Sons, the Electrical Engineers. I have dealt with his correspondence, interviewed callers for him, prepared the agenda and the minutes for the Directors' meetings, and taken verbatim notes at those meetings. My shorthand speed is 120 words per minute and typewriting speed 50 words per minute. I can also operate a telex machine.

My reason for seeking another job is that my present employer is retiring soon and I should like a change.

Yours faithfully,

CATHERINE DOWNS

19 Applying for a Job as a Physiotherapist

SUMMER COTTAGE,

WINTON,

WILTSHIRE.

(postcode)

14th February 19--

Dear Matron,

I should like to apply for the position in your physiotherapy department as advertised in the latest issue of 'Physiotherapy'.

I am 26 years old and trained at Bath County Hospital, qualifying for my MCSP five years ago. I spent two years working at the Thompson School for Physically Handicapped Children and have spent the past three years working in a small private practice in Bath. I have been very happy here but am anxious to widen my experience by working in a general hospital.

I enclose references and very much look forward to hearing from you.

Yours faithfully,

ISABEL DOWNS (MISS)

20 Applying for a Job in a Residential Home

16 ABBEYVILLE ROAD,

EASTBOURNE,

SUSSEX.

(postcode)

9th September 19--

Dear Mrs Winter,

I understand from Dr Micklethwaite that you are looking for a resident Cook/Housekeeper for the Residential Home for the Elderly which you run in Eastbourne.

I am seeking such a post following the death of my previous employer.

I was trained at Langley College of Domestic Science and subsequently did a further year's Advanced Cookery course at the Cordon Bleu School in London. I worked for five years in a small country hotel and was for two years employed in a students' hostel in Cambridge. My most recent work has been with a private family, but I would like to return to the greater challenge of a more demanding post. I am a widow with no family ties and get on well with elderly people. A copy of my references is enclosed.

Perhaps you would be kind enough to send me further details of the position and terms of employment.

Yours sincerely,

M. GRAY (MRS)

21 Applying for a Job as a Packer in a Publishing Firm

16 LEICESTER GROVE,
PUTNEY FIELDS,
LONDON SW14.
5th May 19--

Stephen Williams Esq.,
Ernest Moore Ltd,
20 Shaftesbury Passage,
London WC1.

Dear Mr Williams,

I write to ask if there is any possibility of joining your staff as a junior packer. I am 16 years old and have passed seven subjects at GCE 'O' Level, including English Literature and English Language. I had intended to sit 'A' Levels with a view to going on to university. However, the unemployment situation being what it is, and my father having recently been made redundant, I have decided, if I can, to find a job in publishing now and try to work my way up from the bottom. It has always been my ambition to get into publishing and I had hoped to get a degree which would have qualified me for an editorial position; but circumstances have changed and I feel that I must adapt to them.

I am now at Edwardes Comprehensive School and my headmaster, Mr L. Cooper, knows of my intentions and is quite willing to write a letter of recommendation on my behalf.

My friend, Alan Brett-Smith, who works for J. Sibley P.L.C., suggested

that I write to you. Mr Cooper is prepared to give me time off to attend
an interview, should you be kind enough to grant me one.

Yours sincerely,

MATTHEW WELLS

22 Applying for a Job as a Motor Mechanic

197 FIESTA ROAD,
BOXTON,
LANCS.
(postcode)
15th July 19--

N. G. Watt Esq.,
Moberley Watt Ltd,
Boxton,
Lancs.

Dear Mr Watt,

I am writing to ask if you have any vacancies for a trainee motor
mechanic.

I am 17 years old and left Boxton Comprehensive School last year with
five CSEs including maths, woodwork and technical drawing. I have just
finished a short course in car maintenance at Boxton Technical College
as part of the Youth Opportunities Programme. I have always been
interested in cars and motorbikes, and I service and repair my own
motorcycle.

I enclose references from my headmaster and also from the Head of
Department at the Technical College.

Yours sincerely,

GARY NEWLANDS

23 Applying for a Job as Assistant Matron at a School

THE NURSES' HOME,
NEW ROAD,
LONDON SW10.
20th February 19--

Dear Mrs Bristow,

I have seen your advertisement for an Assistant Matron at Botley

Grange Preparatory School in *The Lady* of the 18th February and I should like to apply for the job.

I am 22 years old and trained for my SEN at New Hospital, London. I passed my finals last June and have continued working at the hospital since then. I enjoy my work, but after 4 years in a hospital environment, I should welcome a change and would very much like to live in the country. I have spent the last six months working on the Children's Ward so feel that my experience is particularly suitable for the job advertised.

I have a week's holiday starting next Monday and would be available for interview at any time that is convenient.

Yours sincerely,
MARY KEATING

24   Applying for a Job as a Gardener

THE COTTAGE,
SIDFORD,
DEVON.
(postcode)
14th November 19--

Dear Lord Dover,

Mrs Jenkins tells me that you are looking for a head gardener for your estate in Cornwall. I should like to apply for the position.

I was trained by the GLC Parks Department and for the past 15 years have been employed by Mr J. C. Williams. I am experienced in all shrub and woodland gardening, wall fruit and vegetables, greenhouse work, maintenance of lawns and driveways and basic care of garden machinery. Although I am very happy working for Mr Williams, I am anxious to extend my experience by working on a larger estate.

Mr Williams is prepared to vouch for my efficiency and to allow me time off for an interview. I look forward to hearing from you.

Yours sincerely,
ERIC JONES

25   A Married Couple Applying for a Job

THE LODGE,
YORK PARK,
WEST YORKS.
(postcode)
7th June 19--

Dear Madam,

I reply to your advertisment for a married couple in this week's copy of 'Job Hunting'.

My wife and I are at present employed by Major and Mrs Johns at the above address. They are shortly moving to Scotland and we are therefore looking for another position. We have had twenty years' experience working together, and between us can offer the services of cook, house-keeper, gardener and handyman. We both have clean driving licences and I can wait at table. We are childless and neither of us smokes.

Should you be interested, Major Johns has kindly said he would be prepared to vouch for us, and we can supply references from previous employers. If you found us suitable for the position I can assure you that we would offer reliable, honest and loyal service.

Yours faithfully,
LESLIE BOWMAN

26   Applying for a Job as a Nanny

FARRIER'S COTTAGE,
HOPETON,
SOMERSET.
(postcode)
19th May 19--

Dear Mrs Andrews,

I should like to reply to your advertisement for a Nanny which I saw in this week's 'Nursery World'.

I am 29 years old, NNEB trained and have a clean driving licence. I have worked both in private families and in a Wandsworth Council Day Nursery. I can supply references and feel that my experience in the day nursery will stand me in good stead when caring for your three little boys.

Perhaps you could let me have further details as to salary, hours and whether you employ other staff. I am at present earning £60 per week.

Yours sincerely,

DAPHNE JOHNSON

27 Applying for a Job as a Companion

47 SHEEP LANE,
EAST SHEEN,
LONDON SW14.
1st June 19—

Dear Madam,

I should like to apply for the job of companion/nurse to an elderly lady as advertised in last night's 'New Standard'.

I am 54 years old, a widow with two grown-up children. Although without nursing qualifications, I have spent the last 13 years nursing my severely arthritic father who died three months ago. I am experienced in household management and have a patient and, I hope, friendly disposition. I enjoy caring for people, can supply character references and am available for interview at your convenience.

Yours faithfully,

NELLIE MORRIS

28 Applying for a Job as a Mother's Help

15 HIGHAM HOUSE,
SEATON ROAD,
LONDON SW11.
10th August 19—

Dear Mrs Sampson,

I saw your advertisement for a Mother's Help in today's 'Times' and would like to apply for the job.

I am 17 years of age and have just left Parksea High School. I am due to start my training as a Children's Nurse at Great Ormond Street Hospital for Sick Children in September next year and would particularly like to spend the intervening year gaining some experience in working with children.

Although I have not worked before, I love children and have younger brothers and sisters. I am quite a good cook and am used to helping around the house. I am a hard worker and eager to learn. A report from my headmistress is enclosed with this letter, and the Vicar of St Mark's Church is willing to vouch for me should you care to write to him.

Yours sincerely,

BEATRICE BONNEY

Letters to and from Sales Representatives

29   From a Firm, Announcing a Call by its Representative

[BUSINESS ADDRESS]

4th January 19--

New Bookshop,
181 Park Road,
London SW11.

Dear Madam,

    Our Mr Harry Walters will be calling upon you on the 10th of the month, when we hope to be favoured with your orders.

Yours faithfully,

for Scott & Homes, Ltd

HUBERT SMITH

Sales Department

30   From a Representative, Announcing a Call

THE SMITH'S ARMS,

WORCESTER.

(postcode)

24th February 19--

Black Mountain Gift Shop,
Willett Way,
Hereford.

Dear Sirs,

    I shall be in Hereford next week and hope to call upon you about 28th

February. I shall have stock rooms at the County Hotel and, as I have a wide range of all our new season's novelties, I hope you will take the opportunity of inspecting them.

I look forward to receiving an order from you which will, I assure you, receive my prompt attention.

Yours faithfully,

PETER LONGVILLE

31 From a Representative to his Sales Manager, Enclosing Orders

YORK HOTEL,
HALIFAX.
(postcode)
4th November 19--

Dear Mr Perkins,

I enclose herewith my weekly report of business done, with the order sheets, and statement of accounts collected.

On Monday I shall be at the Queen's Hotel, Wakefield, and on Thursday at the Waverley Hotel, Bradford.

Business is pretty brisk in the old lines, but I find considerable difficulty in booking orders for the more expensive goods. Traders seem afraid to take risks in view of the unsettled state of the market.

Yours sincerely,

HARRY WALTERS

32 From a Representative, Making Suggestions for Increasing Business

WESTERN HOTEL,
HARROGATE.
(postcode)
1st December 19--

Dear Mr Perkins,

I enclose my weekly report of business done, with the order sheets. On Monday I shall be at the Humber Hotel, Bridlington, for the week.

Business has not been good here, and several of our old customers complained that we do not keep our stock sufficiently up to date. Mr Martin, of --------, whom I have known for many years, showed me a

41

wallet which Messrs ------ & ------- are putting out at £--- a dozen. It looked a superior article to ours at £---. I enclose one for your inspection.

I find everywhere the demand is for smart, up-to-date novelties. The price should be reasonable, but this is less important than a really new line of goods.

Yours sincerely,

HARRY WALTERS

33   From a Representative, Suggesting Special Terms

PRINCES HOTEL,

GEORGE STREET,

BRISTOL.

(postcode)

14th March 19--

Telephone: Bristol 0000

Dear Mr Perkins,

I have had a long interview with Mr Hamilton, the buyer for Land & Bowles. They do a considerable export trade, and Mr Hamilton is much interested in our cheaper leather lines. I think a very large order can be booked here, but there will have to be special terms. He has asked me what we could do in the way of extra discount on an order for 30 gross of the lines priced from £2.50 to £5.00. I have promised to let him know by Thursday, so will you please telephone me on receiving this as to the best offer you can make? The order could be worth over £15,000, and I think a special discount of $7\frac{1}{2}$% cash 30 days, in addition to trade and cash discounts, would secure it. The goods would all be exported and would not compete with traders in this country.

Needless to say, I should not suggest the extra discount if I could secure the order on our usual terms, but I can see that is impossible. Also, if these lines sell well, there is every reason to expect further large repeat orders, possibly on more favourable terms.

Yours sincerely,

HARRY WALTERS

34   To a Representative, Complaining of Business Done

[BUSINESS ADDRESS]
4th December 19--

Dear Mr Walters,

I have noticed that of late that there has been a marked decrease in both the size and the frequency of your orders and would be glad to know if you can offer any explanation. We have had no complaints regarding the quality of our recent lines which seem to be doing very well in other parts of the country. It is most important for us to have regular 'feedback' from our representatives and I should be glad to have your views.

Yours sincerely,

GEOFFREY PERKINS

35   Reply

MOORS HOTEL,
WHITBY.
(postcode)
7th December 19--

Dear Mr Perkins,

I was on the point of writing to you about the situation in my territory when your letter reached me. I am very sorry that you should have occasion to complain of a decrease in my orders, but I think I can assure you that the fault lies neither in myself nor in the firm's products. As you are well aware, the rate of unemployment in this part of the country is above the national average and is increasing all the time. There is a widespread feeling of uncertainty about the future and, in the prevailing atmosphere, traders are naturally unwilling to hold sizeable lines of stock. I have certainly had no complaints about the quality of our merchandise but it has to be said that, in times like these, the public are more and more drawn to inferior Japanese goods which do appreciably undersell our own lines.

Within the next three weeks I shall be covering areas which have not been so badly affected by the current recession and I hope that this will be reflected in my orders. However, as far as the general picture is concerned, the outlook is extremely depressing.

Yours sincerely,

HARRY WALTERS

Letters about Finance

For the sake of brevity *Account* is often written a/c in business correspondence.

When writing to the bank it is helpful to quote the number of one's account, perhaps as a heading to the letter, although it is not strictly necessary.

36 Sending a Cheque in Settlement of an Account

[BUSINESS ADDRESS]
18th March 19--

Dear Sirs,

We have pleasure in enclosing a cheque for £204.90 in full settlement of your account dated 1st March. There is no need to acknowledge receipt.

Yours faithfully,
H. LOUGH
Accountant
For Wilson & Sons

37 Asking for an Overdraft

[BUSINESS ADDRESS]
21st May 19--

a/c No. . . . .
The Manager,
. . . . Bank

Dear Sir,

I enclose a list of orders in hand, all from firms of good repute, including one for over £3000 from the Ministry of Defence. To meet immediate requirements I write to inquire if the Bank will grant me overdraft facilities up to £2000 for a period of six months on the usual terms. I should be obliged if you would let me know if this can be arranged. I shall be pleased to discuss the matter with you, if required.

Yours faithfully.
JOHN CZARKOWSKI

38   Instructing the Bank to Honour a Signature

[BUSINESS ADDRESS]
30th April 19--

The Manager,

. . . . Bank

Dear Sir,

    Will you please note that by a resolution of the Board of Directors (copy attached) Mr A. L. Johnson is now empowered to sign on behalf of the Company instead of Mr B. Wright. A specimen of Mr Johnson's signature is given below for your records.

Yours faithfully,

BRIAN HARRIS

For the
XYZ Company Limited
Secretary   . . . .

Specimen signature of Andrew Leonard Johnson . . . .

39   Requesting Payment Before Delivery of Goods

[BUSINESS ADDRESS]
19th October 19--

Dear Sir,

    The posters ordered by you are ready for delivery. We enclose our invoice and will dispatch them when we have received your remittance.

Yours faithfully,

D. S. LOUGH
pp* Bright P.L.C.

40   Requesting Payment not Due

[BUSINESS ADDRESS]
18th March 19--

Dear Sirs,

    We find that your a/c with us, due for settlement at the end of April, is £---. As a special inducement for immediate settlement, we are willing

per pro (for and on behalf of)

to allow you a special discount of 5%. We should be glad to hear if this proposal is acceptable.

Yours faithfully,
C. T. BONES
Director
C. Morgan & Son

41   Requesting Payment of Account

[BUSINESS ADDRESS]
9th November 19--

Dear Sir,

I wish to call your attention to our a/c rendered in July last for £584.34, which is now considerably overdue. I should be glad to have a cheque at your earliest convenience.

Yours faithfully,
CHESTER MEREDITH
Manager
Accounts Department
Blakeney & Co.

42   Repeating Request for Payment of Account

[BUSINESS ADDRESS]
9th December 19--

a/c dated ---, £---
Dear Sir,

I wrote to you on 9th November asking you to settle your outstanding account of £584.34, first invoiced last July, but so far I have had no reply. I must ask you once more to give the matter your immediate attention and let me have a cheque by return of post.

Yours faithfully,
CHESTER MEREDITH

46

43 Requesting Payment of Account and Threatening Legal Proceedings

[BUSINESS ADDRESS]
2nd January 19--

a/c dated ---, £---

Dear Sir,

I regret to say that this is the last letter I intend to write to you concerning your outstanding account of £584.34. If I do not receive a cheque in full settlement by 12th January, I shall place the matter in the hands of my firm's solicitors. I much regret having to take this course of action, but you leave me with no alternative.

Yours faithfully,

CHESTER MEREDITH

44 Asking for Time in Settling an Account

[BUSINESS ADDRESS]
4th January 19--

Dear Sir,

I regret that your account should have been so long outstanding. I have had very heavy expenses to meet lately and at the same time have been unable to collect several large accounts due to me. In the circumstances I should take it as a great favour if you would allow the account to stand over for a few weeks longer.

Yours faithfully,

K. A. ABAVANA

45 Promising Payment and Deprecating Legal Proceedings

[BUSINESS ADDRESS]
6th January 19--

Dear Sir,

I regret very much that your account has not been paid before this and, I hope, in view of the special circumstances which I explained to your representative, you will not think it necessary to go to the trouble and expense of legal proceedings. I have been pressed by certain creditors lately, but the embarrassment is temporary, and I can promise that your account will be settled at the end of this month, by which date I hope to receive substantial payments from debtors whose accounts are long overdue.

Yours faithfully,
P. D. PETERS

46   Disputing an Account

[BUSINESS ADDRESS]
8th October 19--

Dear Sir,

I regret to say that we are unable to reconcile your statement for September and are returning it herewith. May we bring the following points to your attention:

1 Item 3 Your quotation (Ref GP/1692) was £17.25 per dozen. You have charged £17.75 per dozen.

2 Item 5 You have charged for 8 dozen pairs. We ordered and received only 6 dozen pairs.

3 Item 9 This appears to have been charged in error. We neither ordered nor received the goods and the order number shown is not ours.

Please could you look into these matters and let us have a corrected statement in due course.

Yours faithfully,
MICHAEL HENCHARD
Secretary
Richard Newson Ltd

47   Acknowledging the Receipt of a Cheque

[BUSINESS ADDRESS]
14th June 19--

Dear Sir,

We have pleasure in acknowledging the receipt of your cheque for £--- in settlement of your a/c to 31st May last, and enclose our receipt.

Yours faithfully,
H. P. SLIM
Accountant
Stone & Co., Ltd

48 Disallowing a Discount

Dear Sir,

We have pleasure in acknowledging the receipt of your cheque for £--- in settlement of your a/c to 30th June last, but note that you have deducted $2\frac{1}{2}$% as discount. We regret we cannot allow this. Our terms are $3\frac{1}{2}$% for prompt cash and $2\frac{1}{2}$% on monthly a/cs, and these terms were stated when acknowledging your order, and are printed on our invoices. This account is ten weeks' old, and therefore is not subject to cash discount. We shall be obliged if you will let us have a cheque for the balance, on receipt of which we shall send you a receipt for the full amount.

Yours faithfully,

C.T. Bow

pp C. Morgan & Co. Ltd

49 Requesting Payment to Reduce Debit

Dear Sir,

We thank you for your order for woollen goods (No. L821), but would point out that the debit balance on your a/c is now £2419.60 and exceeds the limit of £2000 to which we agreed. We shall, therefore, be obliged if you will send us a cheque to reduce your debt to us, when we shall be happy to give your order our immediate attention.

Yours faithfully,

C. T. Bow

Secretary

C. Morgan & Co. Ltd

50 Requesting Payment to Avoid Bankruptcy

Personal

Michael Hills Esq.,

Company Secretary,

Frank Waters P.L.C.,

Dear Mr Hills,

I am being hard pressed at the moment by a large creditor who has suddenly called in a debt I had not expected to be asked to pay for some months. This is causing me much embarrassment, and I shall be in grave difficulties unless I can raise £5000. I have orders in hand for you worth over £2000 and, as you have always been satisfied with my work, I venture to ask you if you could let me have a cheque for £1000 on account of the order.

I am extremely sorry to make this request, but I hope you will see your way to oblige me. I shall regard it as a very great favour.

Yours sincerely,

NICHOLAS THOMPSON

Tradesmen's Letters

51 To Wholesalers, Opening an Account

Dear Sirs,

I am shortly opening these premises as a grocery supermarket. I was for many years with George Swains & Co., where I handled your goods, and should like to open a monthly account with you.

Will you please send me your up-to-date catalogue, and let me know what are the best terms you can offer me as to discounts and credit?

I am already known to your Mr Anderson and, if you wish to make any further inquiries, Mr Robson, of George Swains & Co., and Mr J. T.

Brown, of this town, who already deals with you, know me very well. My Bankers are ------- to whom reference can be made.

Yours faithfully,

GEORGE BROWN

52 From Wholesalers, Agreeing to the Opening of a New Account

[BUSINESS ADDRESS]

6th March 19--

Dear Mr Brown,

We thank you for your letter of 1st March and enclose our catalogues. We shall be happy to execute your orders on our usual terms – $2\frac{1}{2}\%$ discount at one month, or $3\frac{1}{2}\%$ for prompt cash – and trust this may be the beginning of a long and mutually profitable connection between us.

Our Mr Allen hopes to call upon you on 12th March, and your orders, passed to him or sent to us direct, will always have our immediate attention. Mr Allen will also be pleased to discuss with you various suggestions concerning window display, circularizing, etc. We like to help our customers in every possible way and hope you will not hesitate to write to us whenever we can be of use.

Yours sincerely,

JAMES ROLLIVER

Director

The Universal Produce Co. Ltd

53 To Wholesalers, Enclosing an Order

[BUSINESS ADDRESS]

8th March 19--

Dear Sirs,

I am very much obliged to you for your letter of 6th March and thank you for your offer of three months' credit.

I enclose an order and look forward to taking delivery at your earliest convenience.

I expect to do an extensive trade here, as there is no other supermarket in the town, and I shall always be pleased to see your representative and to hear of any new lines or special offers.

Yours faithfully,

GEORGE BROWN

54   To a Customer, Acknowledging the Receipt of an Order

[BUSINESS ADDRESS]
14th April 19--

Dear Sir,

Your order of 13th April has been received and is having my immediate attention. I hope to dispatch the goods on Friday next, and I am sure they will give every satisfaction.

I look forward to receiving further orders from you in the future, which, you may rest assured, will receive our immediate attention.

Yours faithfully,

B. K. ONAMA

55   To a Customer, Acknowledging the Receipt of an Order and Offering Alternative Goods

[BUSINESS ADDRESS]
10th May 19--

Dear Sir,

I thank you very much for your order of 28th April, but regret that I am not able to supply the dozen shirts to your pattern. These are last year's stock and are no longer obtainable. I enclose, however, a similar article which I can supply at £49.50 – slightly higher than your instructions for this item. I am dispatching the rest of your order today by Parcel Post, and trust the goods will reach you in good order and give every satisfaction.

Yours faithfully,

JAGDISH PATEL

56　To Wholesalers Asking for a Quotation

[BUSINESS ADDRESS]
8th November 19--

Dear Sirs,

I would be obliged if you would let me know the lowest price you can quote for a good quality China tea for a regular order of ————— per month.

Yours faithfully,

S. T. HUSAIN

57　Another Letter Asking for a Quotation

[BUSINESS ADDRESS]
17th June 19--

Dear Sirs

Would you please quote for manufacturing 5000 booklets similar to the example enclosed.

The new booklet will be increased in length to allow for twelve photographs to be reproduced in varying sizes, but not larger than 10 $7\frac{1}{2}$cm, positioned close to the relevant text. We would supply bromide prints of the subjects.

Copy and illustrations would be ready on acceptance of your price; delivery would be required not more than eight weeks thereafter.

Yours faithfully,

GRAHAM WOODS
pp Paul Montague P.L.C.

58　Acknowledging a Request for a Quotation

[BUSINESS ADDRESS]
19th June 19--

Dear Sir,

Thank you for your inquiry for 5000 booklets. These would be ideally suited to our plant and I hope you will find our work price attractive. Meanwhile, I enclose examples of similar work which we have done so that you may see the standard of quality which we achieve.

Our estimate will reach you in about ten days' time, with samples of the paper which we propose to use.

Yours faithfully,
CHRISTOPHER STEVENSON
Manager
The Crown Printing Press Ltd

59　To a Customer, Refusing Credit

[BUSINESS ADDRESS]
15th May 19--

Dear Madam,

Thank you for your order of the 14th May. I enclose our invoice and will be happy to dispatch the goods immediately on receiving your remittance. I regret that we only do business on a cash basis, as our prices are cut so fine that they do not permit credit terms.

Yours faithfully,
J. A. RAHIN

60　To a Customer, Asking for Payment

[BUSINESS ADDRESS]
28th June 19--

a/c dated ---, £---

Dear Sir,

I am writing to point out to you that it is now eleven weeks since you settled your account. As you know, we do not extend credit facilities beyond eight weeks, so I must ask you to let me have a cheque in respect of goods purchased during at least the first seven weeks of the period in question before you make any further purchases.

Yours faithfully,
R. M. CLARKE

61   To a Customer, Answering his Complaint Regarding the Charges of a Firm

[BUSINESS ADDRESS]
1st September 19--

Dear Sir,

I have received your letter of 29th August and very much regret that you find my charges excessive. When I compare the charges with my own costs, I find myself unable to agree that any item is overcharged. For good work these are fair and reasonable prices.

With regard to the three particular items which you query, these are all for jobs in which skilled labour was employed; possibly you are not aware that good upholsterers are very highly paid. French polishing also requires skilled labour.

In the circumstances, I regret that I am not able to make any reduction, and shall be glad to have your cheque in settlement at your early convenience.

Yours faithfully,

JOHN WATSON

62   Granting Special Terms to a Retailer

[BUSINESS ADDRESS]
2nd May 19--

Dear Sirs,

We have received your letter of 27th April and regret to learn that you have not been able to dispose of our goods as quickly as you had anticipated. We have no doubt that there is still a ready market for the goods, provided they are properly displayed, and we shall be happy, on this occasion, to grant you special credit facilities. We propose to let the March a/c stand over until the end of June and still allow the usual discount.

We must emphasize, however, that this is a special concession which cannot be repeated.

Yours faithfully,

RICHARD CARSTONE
Chief Accountant
Clare & Co. Ltd

63 Asking for References before Opening a New Account

[BUSINESS ADDRESS]
6th March 19--

Dear Sir,

Thank you for your letter of 4th March stating that you wish to open a credit account with us. We are happy to offer the usual facilities but, as this is your first transaction with us, may we trouble you to send us a bank and two trade references?

On hearing from you, we will dispatch our full catalogue, and hope to be favoured with your orders.

Yours faithfully,

A. M. BANKOLE
Director
The Sierra Leone Produce Co. Ltd

64 Making Inquiries about a Customer Wishing to Open an Account

[BUSINESS ADDRESS]
8th March 19--

Private and Confidential

Dear Mr Amis,

Mr Patel, of Park Road, has applied to us to open a credit account and given us your name. We would much appreciate it if you would tell us anything you know of him and his financial standing. Would it, in your opinion, be safe to allow him credit facilities up to £---? Any information you can give us will, of course, be treated in the strictest confidence.

Yours faithfully,

GEORGE BROWN
Director
The London Produce Co. Ltd

65   Reply

Private and Confidential

Dear Mr Brown,

Thank you for your letter of 8th March. I have known Mr Patel for ten years and find him to be a person of good character and integrity. I cannot comment on his financial circumstances, but I would expect him to honour any business undertakings.

It must be understood that this information is given without recourse.

Yours sincerely,

P. Amis
Director
Plastikitsch Ltd

66   To Wholesalers, Complaining of Delay in Delivery

[BUSINESS ADDRESS]
1st December 19--

Dear Sirs,

I must .protest most emphatically about your failure to deliver my order No. 6420. I have now telephoned three times but, in spite of your repeated promises that the goods were about to be dispatched, nothing has arrived. It is causing me the greatest inconvenience and I am losing business as a result; if you cannot let me have the goods immediately, please cancel my order and I will take my business elsewhere.

Yours faithfully,

ROBERTON GARTON
Manager
Garton & Jarman Ltd

67   From Wholesalers, Answering a Complaint of Delay

[BUSINESS ADDRESS]
3rd December 19--

Dear Mr Garton,

We regret very much that we have not been able to execute your order

(No. 6420) as soon as we anticipated. We have had great difficulties in getting our usual supplies from the French shippers, but have now been advised that a large shipment should reach us in two days' time. We have every confidence, therefore, of being able to dispatch the goods to you before the end of this week.

I do apologize for the inconvenience you have been caused.

Yours very sincerely,

FRANK ASHURST
Director
James Galsworthy P.L.C.

68   To a Customer, Answering her Complaint of Delay

[BUSINESS ADDRESS]
19th August 19--

Dear Madam,

I am sorry I have not been able to dispatch the wallpaper ordered by you on 2nd August. I am out of stock of this particular line and, although I have been expecting a delivery from the manufacturers daily, it has not yet been delivered.

I have, however, a very similar paper in stock, of which I enclose a sample. If you care to take this instead, I can dispatch from stock immediately on hearing from you.

I very much regret the inconvenience you have been caused.

Yours faithfully,

GEORGE BROWN
pp Patel & Co.

69   To Wholesalers, Complaining of the Quality of Goods Received

[BUSINESS ADDRESS]
2nd February 19--

Dear Sirs,

We have received the bath towels (our order No. WH69) and must respectfully point out that they are not in any way up to the quality of the sample on which we ordered. If you can allow us a discount of 35% on the price originally quoted, we will keep them. Otherwise I am afraid that we must return the whole consignment. We will hold them in stock until we hear from you.

Yours faithfully,
A. KNIGHT (Mrs)
pp Grieveson P.L.C.

70   From Wholesalers, Answering the Complaint

[BUSINESS ADDRESS]
14th September 19--

Dear Mr Moore,

We have received your letter of 12th September, and are at a loss to understand your complaint as to the quality of the linen supplied to you. This is a line we have sold for years and we have received no complaints from other customers. It is made in our own mills, and the source of the raw material has not been changed. We feel, therefore, that you must be under a misapprehension in thinking the quality is inferior to previous supplies. We are, however, sending our Mr Stanley to inspect the goods and will write to your further when we have received his report.

Yours sincerely,
CYRIL FIELDING
pp Steiner & Co. Ltd

71   From Wholesalers, Answering a Complaint and Refusing to Accept Returned Goods

[BUSINESS ADDRESS]
4th September 19--

Dear Mr Bone,

I write to acknowledge your letter of 1st September. I have thoroughly investigated the complaint you make and, with all due respect, I must say that I do not think it is justified. The slight variation in quality is no more than is usual in this class of goods and certainly no more than you have accepted without complaint in the past.

It is our view that the terms of your order have been fully complied with and in the circumstances I fear that we cannot allow you to return the goods.

Yours sincerely,
ERIC WHITE
Partnership Plastics Ltd

72   To Wholesalers, Notifying Damaged Goods

[BUSINESS ADDRESS]
8th June 19--

Order No. ---, Dated -----.

Dear Sirs,

    The six bales of linen were delivered by British Rail yesterday to the above order but, on opening them, we find that four of the bales have been damaged, apparently before leaving the warehouse, and are quite unsaleable. We are returning them to you by British Rail and shall be obliged if you will replace them or let us have a credit note for their value.

Yours faithfully,
JANET CHIVERS
Manager
C. Allen & Sons

73   To a Customer, Answering a Complaint about Goods

[BUSINESS ADDRESS]
14th July 19--

Dear Sir,

    We very much regret that you should have cause to complain of the condition of the portable cassette recorder supplied by us. We can only imagine that it was damaged in transit as all our goods are inspected before they are packed and dispatched. If you will be good enough to return it to us in its original wrapping, we will send you another at once and refund you the cost of the postage. Please accept our sincere apologies for the trouble you have been caused.

Yours faithfully,
V. R. BISHOP
Manager
Sheepcote Electronics Ltd

74 To an Airline Company, Claiming for Damaged Goods

[BUSINESS ADDRESS]
9th March 19--

The Goods Manager,
Airfreight International Ltd,
Mellstock Airport.

Dear Sir,

Our warehouse manager today accepted from your driver four packages which he signed for as received damaged. We have now examined the contents and enclose herewith a detailed claim. Would you be good enough to arrange for a representative of your company to call at once and inspect the goods.

Yours faithfully,
MATTHEW WELLS
Director

75 To a Railway Company, Re Missing Goods

[BUSINESS ADDRESS]
14th October 19--

The Goods Manager,
British Rail.

Dear Sir,

Twenty crates have been invoiced from James Fenner & Co. of Derby, but only sixteen have been delivered. I have taken the matter up with James Fenner & Co., who inform me that they delivered the twenty crates to Derby Railway Depot on Tuesday, 20th September, and that they hold a receipt from British Rail, signed S.M. Baig. I very much hope that you will be able to trace the four missing crates and deliver them with the minimum possible delay.

Yours faithfully,
H. W. POWELL

76   To a Railway Company, Asking for Special Rates

[BUSINESS ADDRESS]
15th April 19--

The Goods Manager,
British Rail.

Dear Sir,

We are tendering for a very large order, which will entail the carriage of thirty tons of periodicals from these works to London each week. Dispatches would be made each night, and the goods must be collected from these works each afternoon about 4 o'clock. As we have to include cost of carriage in our tender, will you please let us know what is the lowest possible rate you can quote for this.

Yours faithfully,

PETER SANDS
Managing Director
The Acme Printing Co.

77   Advising Shipping Agents of the Dispatch of Goods

[BUSINESS ADDRESS]
2nd March 19--

The Shipping Manager,
United Cargo Containers Ltd,
Sterling Trading Estate,
Park Road South,
Dagenham, Essex.

Dear Sir,

We have today dispatched to you by British Rail 20 (twenty) crates of plastic sandals for shipment at the first available opportunity to Lagos, Nigeria, consigned to A. Ademola & Co. of that port. We enclose herewith delivery note, shipping instructions and three copies of the invoice and would ask you to arrange insurance cover for the amount specified. Please send bills of lading and insurance certificate, together with your account for freight and charges, to ourselves at the above address immediately shipment has been effected.

Yours faithfully,

A. PATEL
George Brown P.L.C.

Letters about Travel

78 To a Travel Agent Asking for Details of a Flight

217 ASH MANSIONS,
PRINCES DRIVE,
LONDON SW11.
5th February 19--

John Service Ltd,
Morning Market,
London W1.

Dear Sirs,

Please will you let me know how I may most conveniently and economically fly from London to Cape Town, allowing stop-over periods of a minimum of 8 (eight) working hours at the following points: Paris, Rabat, Dakar, Lagos, Lusaka. Could you also send me the names of suitable hotels in each city, except Paris, in the price range of £25–£35 per night. I wish to leave London not earlier than 12 noon on Monday 12 April and not later than 12 noon on Wednesday 14 April. Any information regarding visa required, or inoculations, will be most helpful.

I look forward to hearing from you and in due course asking you to make the necessary arrangements on my behalf.

Yours faithfully,
ROBERT STAPLE

79 Booking a Room in a Hotel

THE MILL,
LUNSBY,
ESSEX.
(postcode)
28th August 19--

The Manager,
Lydgate Hotel,
Overcliff,
Dorset.

Dear Sir,

Will you please reserve a single room with bath in my name for one night. I shall be arriving at 1630 hrs on 14 September and hope to leave by 0930 on 15 September.

Yours faithfully,

J. H. JOHNSTONE

80 Booking a Hire Car

728 27th STREET,

MANHATTAN BEACH,

CALIFORNIA 90266,

USA.

16th March 19--

Star Car Hire,
Bedford House,
High Road,
London SW1.

Dear Sirs,

   I shall be arriving at London Airport on Flight BA 282 from Los Angeles at 1335 hrs on Monday 24th March. Would you arrange to have a self-drive four-seater car to await me at the airport. I will check in at your desk as soon as I have cleared customs and immigration.

Yours faithfully,

ROBERT E. CLARK

81 To a Railway Company, Claiming Refund on an Unused Ticket

17 JENNER AVENUE,

LONDON NW8.

19th September 19--

The Manager,
British Rail,
Paddington,
London W2.

Dear Sir,

   On 1st September I took a first-class return ticket from Paddington to Bristol. I have not, however, been able to use the return half, as I was called from Bristol to Manchester and returned to London from there. I enclose the unused half and shall be grateful if you will make a refund.

Yours faithfully,

SAID A. JAWAD

Circular Letters

82 Enclosing New Price-List

[BUSINESS ADDRESS]
19th November 19--

Dear Madam,

We should like to call your attention to the enclosed price-list. We are proud to announce that, through careful buying on a large scale, we have been able to avoid price increases in most of our more popular lines. We would particularly like to draw your attention to Section 12 (household linen) wherein we feel sure you will find many attractive offers at remarkably low prices.

If you are unable to visit us, we hope that you will avail yourself of our 'Shopping by Post' system, full details of which will be found in the enclosed price-list.

Yours faithfully,
Marsh & Brooke P.L.C.

83 On Opening New Premises

Mr T. Mist is proud to announce that he will be opening a new shop at 172 Bell Road, Balham, on 24th April. This is in addition to the present shop in Battersea. The new premises are fitted out with the most up-to-date hygienic equipment and Mr Mist is confident that 'Mist for Fish' will soon be as familiar a slogan in Balham as it has been in Battersea for 50 years.

84 On Opening an Extension of Existing Premises

[BUSINESS ADDRESS]
2nd October 19--

Messrs Watkins and Johnson are pleased to announce the opening on 1st April of the extension to their premises at 100 Sherborne Road, Blackton. The new departments will offer a comprehensive range of beds, bedroom furniture, bed linen and duvets.

You are most cordially invited to attend the official opening of the new building which will be carried out by Councillor Jenkinson at 12 noon on Saturday 1st April.

We much appreciate your past custom and hope that we may continue to have the pleasure of serving you in the future.

85　Offering Special Goods

[BUSINESS ADDRESS]
20th November 19--

Dear Sirs,

We have received advice of a consignment of dolls from our agents in Stuttgart. These are some of the finest models on the market at present and, as we have secured the entire consignment at exceptional prices, we are able to offer them to our customers at a very attractive figure.

We enclose a list giving sizes and prices. If you would like to take advantage of this offer, please inform us at once, as our supply is limited and the offer cannot be repeated.

The consignment is now at the docks, so prompt delivery can be made.

Yours faithfully,
Hallam & Co. Ltd

86　Notifying a Change in Partnership

[BUSINESS ADDRESS]
5th January 19--

Messrs Paterson, Bartlett and Harris announce that Mr Martin Harris will be retiring on 31st March, when the firm will be known as Paterson and Bartlett.

OR

[BUSINESS ADDRESS]
5th January 19--

Dear Sir,

We write to advise you that Mr Jeremy Carlos-Clarke has now been admitted as a partner in this firm, which will in future be known as Martin, Dutton & Carlos-Clarke.

Yours faithfully,
H. MARTIN
G. DUTTON

87   On Taking Over a New Business

[BUSINESS ADDRESS]
19th October 19—

Sir or Madam,

I write to inform you that, on the retirement of Mr T. Jaques, I have taken over the business conducted by him under the name of T. & C. Jaques Ltd.

I propose to trade under the same title and to maintain the firm's high tradition for quality, moderate prices and prompt and courteous service.

May I assure you that your orders will continue to have my best attention.

Yours faithfully,

M. BROWN
(Manager for Messrs T. & C. Jaques for 18 years)

88   Merger Announcement of a Professional Practice

[BUSINESS ADDRESS]
15th December 19—

Dear Mr McCarthy,

Please note that as from 1st January 19— we shall be merging our practice with the old-established city firm of Board, Belcher & Co.

Although the merged firm will have fifteen partners, I assure you that you will still receive personal service from the partner or partners dealing with your affairs, and for the foreseeable future you will be dealing with the same people.

The enlarged firm will be able to offer specialized services such as tax planning, computer advice and management services.

I look forward to our continued association.

Yours sincerely,
A. CRAWFORD

89 Notifying Change of Agent

[BUSINESS ADDRESS]
1st November 19--

Dear Sirs,

We wish to notify you that we have appointed Mr Kenneth Read our sole representative in London, in place of Mr L.P. Stone who is moving to the Midlands for domestic reasons. Mr Read hopes to have the pleasure of calling upon you shortly and will be pleased to help you in any way possible.

Yours faithfully,

J. A. ARNOLD
Managing Director
Arnold & Cook P.L.C.

90 Announcing Change of Manager

[BUSINESS ADDRESS]
16th November 19--

Dear Sirs,

We write to advise you that Mr Harold White gave up his appointment as General Manager on the 15th of this month, when he ceased to be employed by us.

Mr Norman Allen has been appointed to succeed him.

Yours faithfully,

H. L. MOORE
Director
Brown & Sons, Ltd

Social Letters and Letters of Introduction

A formal invitation, ie one in the third person, should receive a formal reply; an informal invitation, an informal reply. Replies to invitations should be answered quickly and should be handwritten.

91 Invitation to a Firm's Staff Dinner

The Directors of
Saltram and Parker Ltd
request the pleasure of the company of

Mr Simon Irvine

at their annual Staff Dinner
to be held at the Morley Rooms, Plymouth Street
on Saturday 15th July at 8 p.m.

RSVP
The Secretary,
100 Brompton Avenue,
Manchester.

92 Acceptance

Mr Simon Irvine has much pleasure in accepting the kind invitation of the Directors of Saltram and Parker Ltd for Saturday 15th July.

93 Refusal

Mr Simon Irvine thanks the Directors of Saltram and Parker Ltd for their kind invitation for Saturday 15th July, but regrets that he is unable to accept owing to a previous engagement.

The President, Sir Bernard Walsh, KBE, and Council of
The National Society of Dendrologists
request the pleasure of the company of

. . . .

at their Tenth Annual Banquet
to be held at the Ritz-Carlton Hotel, Bognor Regis
on Saturday 28th February 19--
at 7.20 for 8.0 p.m.

RSVP
The Secretary,
100 The Parade,
Bognor Regis.

Black Tie

95   Reply Card

Occasionally reply cards, which greatly facilitate the organization of a
large function, are sent out with the invitations.

Serial No: - - - - - -

The Worshipful Company of Sheepshearers' Banquet
Monday, 1st April 198--

Names (s) . . . .

*Has/have much pleasure in accepting the Master's invitation
*Regret(s) being unable to accept the Master's invitation

*Please delete as appropriate

96   To a Colleague on Securing an Appointment

1010 KENYATTA AVENUE,
NAIROBI,
KENYA.
26th January 19--

Dear Ahmed,

    I was delighted to see in the Newsletter that you have been chosen to take over the Mombasa office. Many congratulations on your promotion, which you thoroughly deserve. I know how very busy you must be but I do hope that you will be able to find the time to come and see us before you go.

Yours ever,

JOSEPH

97   To a Senior Colleague on Receiving an Honour

41 VERULAM PLACE,
MANCHESTER.
(postcode)
15th September 19--

Dear Mr Stevens,

    I am writing on behalf of all the staff in 'B' Division to send you our very sincere congratulations on receiving the award of the CMG. You have richly deserved it and it is good to know that your merit has been recognized. We, the members of your own Division, feel particularly proud that you should be so honoured, and we would like you also to accept our very best wishes for the future.

Yours sincerely,

MARK ADAMSON

98   To a Fellow-Officer on his Promotion

6 CHALK HILL,
PORTSMOUTH,
HAMPSHIRE.
(postcode)
10th January 19--

Dear George,

    Very many congratulations on your promotion. It will come as no surprise to those who have served with you and is no more than your due. Nevertheless you must be very pleased as, indeed, I know, are all your friends.

Yours ever,

BILL

99   To a Junior Colleague, Thanking him for his Extra Work

151 LONDON ROAD,
SUTTON COLDFIELD,
WEST MIDLANDS.
(postcode)
5th April 19--

Dear David,

I am extremely grateful to you for looking after Dr Koyama so well during his visit to England. I know that you gave up a great deal of your spare time to do this and assure you that your hard work did not go unappreciated. Indeed it has already proved of considerable value to the firm.

Yours sincerely,

EDWARD FERNEYHURST

100   Acknowledgement

15 ELY ROAD,
CAMBRIDGE.
(postcode)
7th April 19--

Dear Mr Ferneyhurst,

It was very kind of you to take the trouble to write and thank me for looking after Dr Koyama and I am delighted to know that his visit was a success.

I enjoyed his company very much and learned such a lot from him that I hardly feel I deserve the added pleasure which your letter has given me.

Yours sincerely,

DAVID OWEN

101 To a Colleague, Enclosing a Present

74 BRYNMAWR STREET,
CARDIFF.
(postcode)
10th October 19--

Dear Herbert,

I hope that you will accept the enclosed as a token of my gratitude for all the help you have given me during the past three years. Though you, with typical generosity, have always made light of it, I can honestly say that I don't know how I would have survived without your support.

Yours ever,
TOM

102 Thanking

TYTHE BARN COTTAGE,
BRADFORD-ON-AVON,
WILTSHIRE.
(postcode)
15th October 19--

Dear Tom,

Your kind letter and the beautiful cuff-links arrived this morning, and I hasten to say that both are far more than I deserve. Nevertheless I shall always treasure the links as a reminder of the happiness I have derived from our association during the past three years, as indeed I am grateful for the generous but unmerited remarks in your letter.

Yours ever,
HERBERT

103 To a Colleague, Ill in Hospital

414 CHURCH LANE,
PONTRILAS.
(postcode)
3rd May 19--

Dear Barry,

I was extremely sorry to hear that you had been taken to hospital and am writing on behalf of everyone in the office to send you our sympathy and best wishes for a speedy recovery. I will try to visit you in a day or two. In the meantime, I hope that you will let us know if there is anything we can do for you. Don't worry about work. We will manage somehow, much as we miss you.

Yours ever,

ROY

104   To an Employee on the Death of his Wife

72 HARBOUR LANE,
NEWTON ABBOT, DEVON.
(postcode)
24th June 19--

Dear Mr Owen,

I write on behalf of all your friends in the office to send you our heartfelt sympathy on the sudden and tragic death of your wife. Those of us who had the good fortune to know her are all too keenly aware of the great loss you have suffered. If there is anything that any of us can do to help, please don't hesitate to let us know.

Mr Magg is looking after your desk so you have no need to worry on that account, and I shall expect you back when you feel ready to return and not a day before.

Yours, with deepest sympathy,

ALBERT HIGGINS

105   Acknowledgement

88 WEST HILL,
BRIDGWATER, SOMERSET.
(postcode)
30th June 19--

Dear Mr Higgins,

Thank you so much for the kind letter and offer of help which you sent me on behalf of yourself and all my colleagues at the office. I am managing to cope quite well but it means a great deal to me to know that so many friends are thinking of me.

I much appreciate your thoughtfulness in telling me not to hurry back to the office but I'm sure that my work will do much to stop me brooding over what has happened.

With many thanks,

Yours sincerely,

FRANK OWEN

106   To a Business Acquaintance, Announcing the Death of a Colleague

[BUSINESS ADDRESS]

4th February 19--

Dear Mr Long,

It is with great sadness that I write to inform you of the sudden death of Norman Martyn. He had a severe stroke on Friday night and died before he reached hospital. The funeral is private but there is to be a memorial service, of which I will send you details in due course.

Norman's death will inevitably involve some readjustment of our sales force; but I will make it my responsibility to see that the excellent relationship which exists between our companies and for which, I'm sure you will agree, much of the credit belongs to Norman, is not impaired.

Yours sincerely,

THOMAS FOY

Managing Director

107   From a Widow, Announcing the Death of her Husband to his Late Employers

6 CHESTER ROAD,

PENY-BONT,

ANGLESEY.

(postcode)

8th July 19--

The Chairman,
Messrs Paget and Morgan,
Marine Parade,
Anglesey.

Dear Mr Paget,

I am sorry to have to inform you that my husband died in hospital last night after a long illness. The funeral will take place at 2.30 p.m. on

Friday 13th July at Broadfield Cemetery. I would be most grateful if you could tell any of his former colleagues who may like to attend.

Yours sincerely,

ALISON VAUGHAN

108   Asking for a Letter of Introduction

135 BREWERY LANE,
EAST BERGHOLT,
SUFFOLK.
(postcode)
10th May 19--

Dear Mr Churchill,

   I have just heard that I am to go to Manchester next week. I wonder if you would be kind enough to give me a letter of introduction to Professor Satinoff. You mentioned last week that he might be interested in my project, and I should very much like to discuss it with him. Please forgive me for troubling you.

Yours sincerely,

PAUL ADDISON

109   A Letter of Introduction

215 CASTLE STREET,
EDINBURGH,
SCOTLAND.
(postcode)
12th May 19--

Dear Professor Satinoff,

   This is to introduce Paul Addison who studied under me last year and showed great promise. He is, at the moment, working on a project that will, I think, be of interest to you. I should very much appreciate it if you would spare the time to see him.

Yours sincerely,

CRAIG CHURCHILL

110 Introducing a Young Man for Business Purposes

51 FLOOD STREET,
COLCHESTER,
ESSEX.
(postcode)
5th November 19--

Dear Bill,

I wonder if you can help me. A young man called Peter Kent, the son of some friends of ours, has a business project which he wants to discuss with someone experienced in such matters and, as I'm sure you will readily agree, I am hardly the most suitable person! Would you mind very much if he came and saw you? I will tell him that he is not to take up too much of your time; and it is even possible that the idea may be of some interest to you. If you could spare him a few minutes I would be most grateful.

Yours ever,
DAVID

111 Asking a Friend for an Interview for Business Purposes

17 SCRIBE STREET,
BRIGHTON,
SUSSEX.
(postcode)
18th July 19--

Dear Cecil,

I wonder if you could possibly help me. The son of a friend of my wife's is looking for a job in the newspaper world. I gather that he had a few articles published in provincial newspapers while he was at university and now he wants to take Fleet Street by storm. Actually he is a bright and modest boy, and fully realizes that he will have to start at the bottom. Could I possibly send him along to have a chat with you? There can be few people who know their way about the world of journalism better than you.

Yours ever,
BILL

112   Favourable Reply

81 HARMSWORTH HOUSE,
YORK STREET,
LONDON WC1.
20th July 19--

Dear Bill,

How very nice to hear from you! Of course I will see the young man. You didn't mention his name but if he rings my secretary and explains who he is she will fix up an appointment for him. I'll certainly do my best to help him.

Yours ever,
CECIL

113   Less Favourable Reply

81 HARMSWORTH HOUSE,
YORK STREET,
LONDON WC1.
20th July 19--

Dear Bill,

I'll certainly see the young man and have a chat with him, but I don't need to tell you that things are at a pretty low ebb in the world of journalism at the moment. Anyway, send him along and I'll see what I can do.

Yours ever,
CECIL

114   Refusal

81 HARMSWORTH HOUSE,
YORK STREET,
LONDON WC1.
20th July 19--

Dear Bill,

Frankly it would be a waste of both my own and the young man's time if he were to come and see me. The dole queues are swollen with journalists with years of experience and nobody is even hiring tea-boys at the moment. Can't your wife persuade him to become a fashionable hairdresser? He'll get far richer than he ever would in Fleet Street.

Yours ever,

CECIL

115 Introducing a Friend for Business Purposes

17b LILLIE ROAD,
COLCHESTER,
ESSEX.
(postcode)
20th July 19--

Dear Mr Barrymore,

A friend of mine, Richard Evans, would very much like a chat with you. He is at present working on magazines, and is thinking of changing over to newspaper work, and would like to discuss what prospects such work holds out.

I have known him for several years, and find him a delightful friend, intelligent, hard-working and sociable. I think you would enjoy a chat with him, and I know you could give him valuable help and advice. He has sent me a note of his qualifications which I enclose.

I would highly appreciate it if you could find time to see Mr Evans, although I know how busy you are these days.

Yours very sincerely,

ROBERT BARKER

116 Letter of Thanks to a Wife who has Put up a Business Colleague of Her Husband's

15 MONK'S WALK,
LONDON SW3.
20th July 19--

Dear Mrs Bradshaw,

I really am extremely grateful to you for asking me to stay. Your kindness and hospitality made all the difference in the world to my visit to Bradford and I look back with real pleasure on what would otherwise have been a routine business trip.

My warmest thanks to you and your husband.

> Yours,
>
> THOMAS ROBERTS

117 Refusing an Invitation to Stay With a Business Acquaintance

> 15 MONKS WALK,
> LONDON SW3.
> *29th July 19--*

Dear Mr Bradshaw,

How very kind of you and your wife to ask me to stay when I am in Bradford next week. I fear, however, that I must regretfully decline you offer as I have a number of evening engagements and would not like to abuse your hospitality by using you as a hotel! I will, of course, ring you as soon as I arrive and much look forward to seeing you both. Again many thanks.

> With best wishes,
>
> Yours,
>
> THOMAS ROBERTS

Glossary of Business Terms

Account Sales   An account rendered at periodical intervals by the consignee to the consignor showing goods received, sales, expenses incurred, commission charged, and remittances made, with the resultant balance due by him.

Accounts Current   Statements of accounts rendered between home firms and foreign firms, between whom there are frequent transactions, showing the daily balance and adding or deducting interest thereon.

Administrator   Person appointed to administer the estate of a person who dies without leaving a will, or in the following circumstances: (*a*) Where the Administrator undertakes the duty for the purpose of litigation only.   (*b*) Where the deceased's will does not name an Executor, or the Executor named is unwilling to act.   (*c*) Where the original Executor or Administrator has died without completing the distribution of the deceased's estate.

Ad Valorem   According to value.

After Sight   A term used to indicate that the period for which a Bill of Exchange is drawn will not begin until after it has been presented to the drawee.

Agency   The relationship where one person (the agent) acts on the behalf of another (the principal) in such a way as to affect the legal relations between the principal and a third party particularly by making contracts or by dealing in property on his behalf.

Annual Return   This is the Return which every Company which has a share capital must send to the Registrar of Companies. It must include the address of the Company, the place where a list of members is kept, the balance sheet, and a copy of the Auditors' and Directors' Reports. It must be signed by a Director and the Secretary, and submitted within 42 days of the Annual Meeting.

Articles of Association This document defines the powers, rights, duties, and authority of the shareholders and the directors of a Limited Liability Company, and sets out the rights of the Company. It is a set of rules for the internal management of the Company. It is binding on all members and can only be altered by a special resolution of the members.

Auction A method of sale by which intending purchasers state the price they would offer. A sale by auction is complete when the auctioneer announces its completion by the fall of the hammer or in other customary manner. Until such an announcement is made, any bidder may retract his bid.

Auditor He is an accountant qualified by examination or experience, appointed by a company or a business to check the financial records and accounts, and to report to the shareholders or proprietors as to whether the accounts and other financial statements show a true and fair view of the profit or loss for the year, and the state of its affairs at the Balance Sheet date.

Bailee A person (other than a servant) who receives possession of a thing from another and consents to hold it on an undertaking to keep or return or deliver up to the legal owner or to use it or convey it to another in accordance with the owner's directions. Examples are hire, custody, carriage, pledge loan for use, handing over for repair.

Bank Note At one time bank notes were issued by all banks of issue, but now the Bank of England has a monopoly. They are promissory notes payable on demand to bearer, and Bank of England notes are legal tender in Britain. £50, £20, £10, £5 and £1 notes are the only notes now issued in England.

Bankruptcy is a condition of insolvency in which the effects of a man unable to pay his debts are taken over by a trustee and distributed for the benefit of all his creditors. The debtor, or a creditor for not less than £50, must file a petition in the Bankruptcy Court, which makes a receiving order and appoints an Official Receiver to act as trustee until the creditors meet and either confirm his appointment or elect another trustee. At any time a bankrupt may apply to the court for his discharge, and, if this is granted, he is released from his debts. An *undischarged bankrupt* commits a misdemeanour if he obtains credit for £10 and upwards without disclosing the fact that he is an undischarged bankrupt.

Bill of Entry A document describing goods before they are landed, which importers give to the Customs authorities.

Bill of Exchange A bill of exchange is an unconditional order in writing, addressed by one person to another, signed by the person giving it, requiring the person to whom it is addressed to pay on demand or at some future time a sum in money to, or to the order of, a specified person or bearer. The maker of the bill is called the *drawer*; the person to whom it is addressed the *drawee*; the person to whom the money is to be paid the *payee*. In practice the drawer and payee are often the same. A bill of exchange must be *accepted* by the drawee and this is done by writing 'Accepted' across the face, with the date and the signature of the acceptor. *Qualified Acceptance* is one in which the acceptor takes liability for only a part of the sum stated. *Dishonouring a Bill* – failure to pay when due. *Discounting a Bill* – buying a bill of exchange for a less amount than the sum stated. *Retiring a Bill* – discharging it before it is due.

Bill of Lading (B/L) A contract between a shipowner and a shipper to convey specified goods to a specified destination on payment of freight. They are usually drawn up in sets of three, and must be signed by the master of the ship. They are then handed to the shipper.

Board of Trade The central government department, authorized under the Companies Act 1948, to supervise work relating to the organization, recognition and general conduct of companies.

Bond A document by which a person guarantees the fulfilment of a contract, or the integrity of a person.

Bonded Vaults and Warehouses Places where goods subject to duties can be stored.

Broker An agent who buys and sells for other people without taking possession of the goods. He has no authority to sell goods in his own name. *Brokerage* – the remuneration paid to a broker, usually a percentage.

Capital The sum of money employed by a person or Company in a business undertaking. The principal of a loan. In a partnership firm, Capital is the excess of assets over liabilities; in a Limited Company, the amount stated in the Memorandum of Association which is called the 'authorized' or 'nominal' Capital. *Issued Capital* is the amount issued to shareholders in response to their application for shares, and is often called 'subscribed' Capital. *Paid-up Capital* is the amount actually subscribed for and paid up by the shareholders. Capital in a Limited Company is divided into various other classes also, and the rights of each are determined by the Memorandum of Association or the Articles of the Company.

Charter Party   A document which sets forth the agreement between parties in hiring a ship for a voyage or for a period.

Cheque   A cheque is a bill of exchange payable on demand, drawn on a banker. *A bearer cheque* is made payable to payee 'or bearer' and does not require endorsement by the payee. An *order cheque* is made payable to payee 'or order' and if presented at the counter of the bank on which it is drawn will require endorsement by the payee. A *crossed cheque* is a cheque payable either to bearer or to order, on which two parallel lines have been drawn across the face; sometimes the words '& Co.' are placed within the lines. It must be presented for payment to the bank on which it is drawn by a banker, and can only be collected through a banking account. If the name of a particular bank is added to the crossing, payment will only be made into that bank, and if a particular account at a particular bank is specified in the crossing then a collecting banker may only collect it for that account. It is not necessary to endorse cheques drawn on a bank within the United Kingdom which are paid in to the account of the payee, but an order cheque negotiated by the payee to a third party still requires endorsement. A *post-dated* cheque is one which bears a future date and it will not be paid before that date. A *stale cheque* is one that has not been presented for payment within a reasonable time. Most banks refuse to pay after six months. (See also Endorsement.)

Circular Note   A letter of credit issued by a bank to clients enabling the holders to obtain payment at various places abroad.

Commission   The remuneration paid to an agent for carrying through a transaction or introducing business. Thus stockbrokers, estate agents, auctioneers, etc., are paid a commission for work done, usually in the form of a percentage. A commercial traveller is often paid a commission in the form of a percentage of the value of orders secured.

Company   One registered under one of the Companies Acts. It is an association of persons combined for purposes of profit, and contributing to a common capital. The legal provisions which govern the formation of companies are controlled by the Companies Acts of 1948, 1967, 1980 and 1981. A Company can either be a public or a private one; a *Private Company* need only have two members, a *Public Company*, seven. A *Limited Company* is one where each shareholder's financial liability is limited by the number of shares he holds, ie in case of bankruptcy he can be made to contribute only to the value of his own individual shareholding. A *Public Limited Company* must include the term 'Public Limited Company' on the accepted abbreviation 'P.L.C.' (in upper or lower case) at the end of its name.

Cover   Money deposited as security against possible loss.

Cover Note   A document issued by insurers giving temporary insurance cover pending the issue of a formal insurance policy.

Credit (Cr.)   In book-keeping the credit side of an a/c is the one on which receipts are entered. The word is also used to mean a sum of money owing to you; the time allowed for payment of an a/c; and the confidence felt in your ability to pay.

Credit, Letter of   A letter given to anyone, addressed to a banker, instructing the banker to meet the drafts of the person nominated in the letter up to a certain figure. A *Circular Letter of Credit* is a letter usually issued by a bank to its branches or agents in several places for the same purpose.

Credit Note   A form, usually printed in red ink, in which is given the amount of a reduction or rebate in an a/c already rendered.

Credit Sale   An agreement for the sale of goods under which the price is payable by five or more instalments, not being a conditional sale agreement.

Creditor   One who has a claim for money upon you.

Current Account   The a/c with a bank which is used for the ordinary business routine of collecting and paying a/cs. Interest is not usually allowed on a current a/c, and if the balance maintained is small a charge is made by the bank for working the a/c. (See *Deposit a/c.*)

Customs Duties   The taxes levied on certain imported and exported goods.

Days of Grace   Extra time allowed by law or custom for making certain payments. Thus 3 days are allowed in meeting a bill of exchange, 15 days in paying the premium on a fire insurance policy, and 30 days in paying the premium on a life insurance policy.

Debenture   A document issued under the Seal of the Company, usually charging all or some of a Company's property in favour of the holder. It provides for interest to be paid, and usually for the time of repayment of the Capital sum. A debenture is the instrument acknowledging the debt. A *Mortgage Debenture* is one giving a charge on the Company's assets.

Debit   In book-keeping the debit side of an a/c is the one on which outgoings are entered. It also means an amount owing, or debt.

Debtor (Dr)   One who owes.

Demurrage   A charge made for detaining railway trucks beyond a specified time, or for retaining a hired ship after the time fixed by the contract.

Deposit Account   An a/c with a bank into which is paid money not required for immediate use. Interest is paid on it by the bank, and notice of withdrawal is usually required. (See *Current a/c.*)

Directors   Members of a Company responsible for its general policy. Only one director is required, providing that another person is secretary. The directors, or director and secretary, are named in the Articles, or in the Memorandum of Association, or are appointed by the Company. The functions of directors are exercised collectively rather than individually.

Discount   A deduction, usually a percentage, allowed from a sum due. *Cash Discount* is allowed for prompt payment. *Trade Discount* is an allowance by a manufacturer or a wholesaler to a retailer from catalogue prices and is intended to form the retailer's profit. *Special Discount* is allowed for special circumstances, such as exceptionally large orders, or taking soiled or old stock.

Dividend Interest paid on investments. Profits divided among members of a Company in proportion to their shares. *In bankruptcy*: the sum paid per £ out to creditors from the estate of the bankrupt or out of his assets.

Drawback On Excise and Customs duties, a drawback is the return of duties paid – in Excise, when duties have been paid on goods that are being exported; in Customs, when duties have been paid on imported goods which are being exported.

Endorsement The signature of the payee on a cheque or any other document drawn to a person's order.

Endowment Policy See Insurance.

Excise Duties Taxes levied by the Government on certain articles manufactured for home consumption.

Executor (*fem.* **Executrix**) Person appointed by a will to see that its provisions are carried out.

Factor An agent entrusted with the possession of goods for the purposes of sale.

First of Exchange Bills of exchange on firms abroad are often drawn in triplicate for safety. The first and second are forwarded by different mails and the third retained. If the first is met, the second and third are valueless.

Hypothecation The pledging of goods or a ship. It differs from pawning in that the goods themselves are not given up. *A Letter of Hypothecation* is a printed form addressed to a bank authorizing them to sell specified goods if the bill drawn on them is not honoured.

Incorporation This is effected by lodging with the Registrar of Companies the Memorandum of Association, the Articles of Association, a statement of the nominal capital, a list of directors and a statutory declaration of compliance with the Companies Acts of 1948, 1967 and 1980.

Indent A requisition for stores. Also an order for goods.

Inscribed Stock   Company or Government stock for which no certificates are issued.

Insurance   is the way to spread over many losses which would have to be otherwise personally met by the individual. It is a pool to which many contribute and out of which those who suffer are compensated. There are various kinds of insurers, the principal being – (*a*) Company insurers, (*b*) Lloyd's Underwriters, (*c*) Mutual insurers. The chief types of insurance are – (*a*) Marine, (*b*) Fire, (*c*) Life, (*d*) Accident (see Third Party). Any class of insurance is possible, provided the assured has an insurable interest in the object insured, ie a financial loss could be sustained. It is a contract to pay on the happening of some event a sum of money to the insured. The contract is called the *Policy of Insurance*, the person insured is called the *assured* or the *insured*, and the person who insures is called the *insurer* or the *underwriter*.

Some Types of Polices: Joint Life Policy is taken out on the lives of two persons under the one policy, eg on the joint lives of husband and wife, when the policy money is usually payable to the survivor on the death of the other. The premium is higher than for an ordinary single life policy. *Life Policy* is a contract on the person whose life is assured, under which the policy money is payable at his death (*Whole Life Assurance*): or a contract engaging to pay at maturity or at death, whichever shall occur first (*Endowment Assurance*). The 'assured' and the 'life assured' may be different persons, but there must be what is termed 'an insurable interest'. *Life Policy, Short Term*, is taken out usually for some special purpose, eg business trips abroad; the sum assured is payable only in the event of the death of the assured. *Marine Policies*: These are contracts against losses incident to accidents at sea to ships, cargo, etc., for a given voyage or voyages, or during a certain length of time. The contract is usually made through brokers, who are responsible to the underwriters for the premium. *Types of Marine Policies*: An *Open* policy does not state the value of the goods insured, and after loss this has to be settled. A *Valued* policy fixes this beforehand and it is stated in the policy. Insurers should be careful to insure for all risks, and, if necessary, from warehouse to warehouse.

Surrender Value is the amount paid by the insurers in consideration for the cancellation of an insurance policy.

Inter Alia   Among other things.

Interest   Money paid for the use of money, usually calculated at a certain rate per cent per annum. *Simple Interest* is charged on the sum lent only. *Compound Interest* is charged on the sum lent and on interest which has accrued and remains unpaid.

Invoice   A form giving particulars of goods which have been dispatched to a customer, with prices and charges. *Pro Forma* invoice – one that is sent before the goods have been dispatched, usually to indicate that payment in advance is required.

IOU (Contraction of 'I owe you')   An acknowledgement of a debt. It requires no stamp.

Jerquer   A Customs official who searches ships for dutiable articles and checks ships' papers relating to import goods. *Jerquer Note* – given by Customs' officer to the master of a ship to certify that he has inspected the vessel.

Legal Tender   Money which a creditor is legally bound to accept in payment of a debt. In England legal tender is currency notes up to any amount, silver or cupro-nickel coins; 50p and 20p up to £10, and 10p and 5p up to £5; decimal bronze up to 20p.

Liens   are of various kinds – possessory, maritime, equitable. The first relates to a person who holds the goods and property which belong to another, and is entitled to retain them until he is paid what is due to him; the second is a lien which arises from a liability in regard to a maritime mishap, it does not depend on the actual possession of the property; the third lien is the granting of part of the property to be allocated to the payment of a specific liability. Liens are, in fact, the right to possession or retention pending settlement of a debt.

Life Policy   See Insurance.

Limited Liability Company   See Company.

Liquidation   Realizing and distributing the assets of a Company (see Winding-up).

Lloyd's   started as a coffee-house in 1687, frequented by ship-owners and seafaring men. It was a kind of club. It developed into a market and became eventually the world centre for insurance of ships and cargoes. If a person insures at Lloyd's he places the risk not with Lloyd's itself, but with one or more of the syndicates of Lloyd's Underwriters, and every member of the syndicate is directly responsible to the insured for his share of any loss. Business has to be done through a Lloyd's broker, who places the risk with the underwriters (see Underwriters) and distributes the premiums. He also collects the claims for his principal. Practically all kinds of insurance may now be effected at Lloyd's.

Memorandum of Association   A document setting forth the name, address, objects and powers, the limitation of members' liability, and the share capital of a Company. It is the Company's charter defining and limiting its field of operations. In the case of a Public Company seven of the members must sign; in the case of a Private Company, two. (See Company.)

Mortgage   A deed by which a person assigns property to another as security for a sum of money lent. A pledge as security for a debt. A *Mortgagee* – a person to whom the mortgage is given; a *Mortgagor* – a person who gives the mortgage.

On Call   Money lent is said to be on call when it must be repaid on demand or at short notice.

Overdraft   Overdrawing is an act by which more is withdrawn from a bank than has actually been placed there by the individual or Company concerned. The overdraft is the amount by which a banker allows a customer to meet debts in excess of the customer's holdings in the bank.

Owner's Risk   Railway Companies convey goods at reduced charges at owner's risk, which means that they are not responsible for loss or damage except that caused by wilful misconduct of their servants.

Par   Face value.

Partnership   An association of not fewer than two and not more than twenty persons for business purposes, sharing risks and profits. *Sleeping partner* – one who contributes capital to the business but takes no actual share in its management.

Patents   A patent is a grant from the Crown of 'letters patent' to an inventor of some manner of new manufacture, conferring on him the sole rights in his invention. Patents last for 14 years. Fees are payable on application, and each year after the fourth year. Applications must be made to the Patent Office, Southampton Buildings, Chancery Lane, London WC2. A *Patent Agent* undertakes to prepare and make applications, and must be registered.

Per Pro (pp)   On behalf of. Used when signing on behalf of a firm or another person.

Probate   is the official copy of a will with the seal or certificate of the Probate Court, showing that it has been duly proved. The grant of probate enables the executor to deal with the estate.

Promissory Note   is an unconditional promise in writing made by one person to another signed by the maker, engaging to pay on demand or at some fixed determinable future date a sum in money to, or to the order of, a specified person. If payable to order it must be endorsed by the payee.

Public Limited Company (P.L.C.)   As a result of the 1980 Act, all Public Companies having a share capital must substitute 'P.L.C.' or 'Public Limited Company' for their previous designation.

Quorum   The minimum number of people who must be present at a meeting to allow business to be conducted.

Receipt   Formal acknowledgement that goods or money have been received.

Remittance   That which is sent, ie the sending of money, etc., to a distance.

Shares   The capital of a Company is often divided into *Ordinary, Preference*, and *Deferred Shares*. Preference Shares entitle the holder to receive a dividend from the profits of the Company at a fixed rate per cent, and this must be paid before anything is paid to the holders of Ordinary Shares. With *Cumulative* Preference Shares, any arrears of dividend must also be paid before the ordinary shareholders can participate in the profits. *Deferred* Shares are the exact opposite of Preference Shares, and cannot participate in profits until all other dividends have been paid. In the event of the distribution of the assets of the Company, the same order of precedence among the different classes of shareholders is observed. (See also Stocks and Debentures.)

Short Term Policy   See Insurance.

Sine Die   Without a day being named – indefinitely.

Statute-barred   Barred by the Statute of Limitations.

Statute of Limitations   An Act of Parliament of 1939 which prevents legal actions being brought to recover debts which have been dormant for a number of years. Actions for breach of contract are barred after 6 years and actions on deeds after 12 years.

Stocks   differ from shares only in that they must be fully paid up and can be divided. Shares are not always fully paid up and cannot be divided. Money lent to the Government at interest is called Stock.

Surrender Value   See Insurance.

Tare   In railway and freight charges, an allowance made for the weight of crate, box, or vehicle containing the goods.

Third Party Risks   In insurance, the risk of the policy-holder suffering loss by the act of a third party – ie other than the policy-holder or the Company. Thus fidelity guarantee policies, which insure the employer against loss by the dishonesty of his employee, deal with a third party risk.

Trade Mark   A distinguishing mark placed on goods for trade purposes and registered at the Patent Office. Registration is valid for 14 years, as provided for by the Trade Marks Act 1938.

Transfer Days   The days on which the Bank of England enters in its books the transfers of Government stock without charge.

Transire   Permit granted by the Customs authorities for the removal of goods.

Trustee One to whom property has been conveyed or bequeathed to apply for the purposes directed by the trust. A trustee can be appointed by deed or will, by an order of the Court of Chancery, and in bankruptcy proceedings.

Trustee Investments Trustees are limited by Act of Parliament to certain classes of stock when investing funds in their charge, and these are known as Trustee Investments; also as Gilt-Edged Securities.

Turnover Gross output of a business.

Underwriters Persons who undertake to buy the shares or a specified number of shares which are not taken up when a new issue of shares in a Limited Liability Company is made. In *shipping circles* underwriters are members of Lloyd's (see p. 89) who undertake the insurance of ships and cargoes. In general terms, to underwrite is to subscribe one's name to a policy and to become answerable for loss or damage.

Unfunded Debt Loans made to the Government to be repaid at short notice.

Usufruct In law, the temporary use and enjoyment of lands and tenements, or the right of receiving the fruits and profits of land, or other things, without having the right to alienate or change the property.

Usury Lending money at exorbitant rate of interest.

Vendors' Shares The shares in a Company which have usually been allotted to the owners of the business that has been sold to the Company.

Warrant This word is used in a variety of ways. A *Dividend Warrant* is an authorization to receive money. A *Customs Warrant* is an authority to release goods on board ship. A warrant may also be a guarantee of quality, a receipt for goods deposited, an order for arrest, and the grant of a commission (as in the Army).

Waybill A document issued by a railway company, or carrier, giving particulars of goods being carried.

Winding-up The process by which a Company is brought to an end. A petition may be presented to the court which appoints a liquidator to realize the assets and pay the debts of the Company. In a *Voluntary Winding-up* the liquidator is appointed by the Company and/or the Creditors and the court does not intervene except for special reasons.

Without Reserve   All goods sold at auction without a minimum price being fixed are sold 'without reserve'.

PART TWO:

The Domestic Letter Writer

Model Letters

Invitations, Acceptances, Refusals, Letters of Thanks

Letters to Solicitors

Letters about Housing

Letters about Insurance

Letters to Tradesmen

Letters about Education

References and Introductions

Letters about Travel and Holidays

MODEL LETTERS

Invitations, Acceptances, Refusals, Letters of Thanks

118 Formal Invitation to a Dinner Party

Mr & Mrs Denis Milne

Sir Derek and Lady Childs
request the pleasure of your company
at Dinner
on Friday, 9th March
at 8 for 8.30

RSVP
470 Clarendon Road,
London SE11.   Black tie

---

119 Formal Acceptance of Invitation

Mr and Mrs Denis Milne have much pleasure in accepting the kind invitation of Sir Derek and Lady Childs for Friday 9th March.

OR

Mr and Mrs Denis Milne thank Sir Derek and Lady Childs for their kind invitation for Friday, 9th March, which they have much pleasure in accepting.

120   Formal Refusal of Invitation

Mr and Mrs Denis Milne much regret that they are unable to accept the kind invitation of Sir Derek and Lady Childs for Friday 9th March owing to a previous engagement.

121   Formal Invitation to a Dance or Cocktail Party

Commander and Mrs Masters

Mrs Anne Thomas
at Home
Tuesday, 7th June

RSVP
Battleships,
Shoreham,
Sussex.

Dancing
10.30 p.m.

Miss Patricia Wilde

Miss Winifred Neale
at Home

RSVP
The Paddock,
Newfield,
Berks.

Cocktails
6.30 p.m.

122 Informal Invitation to a Party

4 St Dominic Place,
London W1.
8th September 19--

Dear Mrs Draper,

We are having a small supper party on Friday, 18th September, starting about 8 o'clock, and would be so pleased if you and your husband could come. We do hope that you are free that evening and very much look forward to seeing you again.

Yours sincerely,
ALISON DUNN

123 Accepting

2 Crescent Street,
London W1.
11th September 19--

Dear Mrs Dunn,

Thank you very much indeed for your kind invitation, which Norman and I have great pleasure in accepting. We much look forward to seeing you and your husband on the 18th.

Yours sincerely,
ELIZABETH DRAPER

124 Informal Invitation to Dinner

28 Bude Street,
London SW1.
18th November 19--

My dear Laura,

We should be delighted if you could come and dine on Friday, 28th November. Don't bother to dress up. We are just asking a few close friends, most of whom you know. Come at about 7.30 if you are free.

Love from
BERYL

125   Declining

CRESCENT COURT,
LONDON SE1.
20th November 19--

My dear Beryl,

Sadly I must refuse your very kind invitation to dinner on Friday, 28th November. The Gouldens have asked me to stay for the week-end and are calling for me at 7 p.m. It was sweet of you to ask me and I hope that I shall see you both again very soon.

Much love,

LAURA

126   Invitation to a Daughter's Twenty-first Birthday Party

Mr and Mrs Nicholas Thompson request the pleasure of the company of . . . . on Saturday, 1st June, on the occasion of the 21st birthday of their daughter Marilyn.

RSVP
The Cedars,
Surbiton Avenue,
Crawley, Sussex.   Disco 8.30 p.m.

127   Invitation to a Firm's Staff Dance

10 CHAMBERLAIN STREET,
BOXTON,
KENT.
(postcode)
25th July 19--

My dear Catherine,

If you are free on 6th August, would you like to be my guest at my firm's annual staff dinner/dance? As you know quite a number of my colleagues, I think that you would enjoy the evening and it would certainly give me great pleasure to take you. If you are free that evening and would like to come, I suggest that I call for you at about 8.30. Incidentally, I think you should wear a long dress.

With love from

TIMOTHY

128 Accepting

14 EGLISTON TERRACE,

PENSHURST, KENT.

(postcode)

28th July 19--

Dear Timothy,

Thank you very much indeed for your kind invitation. I am flattered that you should ask me to be your guest at your firm's annual party and should love to come with you. I look forward very much to seeing you on the 6th.

Love from

CATHERINE

129 Thanking

14 EGLISTON TERRACE,

PENSHURST,

KENT.

(postcode)

30th July 19--

Dear Timothy,

Thank you very much for a wonderful evening. I enjoyed every minute and I thought that the party was a great success, which I've no doubt was largely due to all the hard work you did in organizing it.

I hope that you will come and have supper here soon. It will seem rather modest after a party as splendid as last Saturday's, but it would be very nice to see you.

Love from

CATHERINE

130 Invitation to a Dinner and Theatre Party

17 PALMER ROAD,
LONDON SW3.
27th April 19--

Dear Sandy,

I tried to telephone you today but could get no answer. I wonder if you are free next Thursday evening and would care to come to the theatre with me and a couple of friends. We are going to see Soyinka's 'Madmen and Specialists', which is on at the Avenue Theatre. Meet me, if you can, in the foyer at 7.15. We'll dine after the play and I'll drive you home.

Love,

CHESTER

131 Accepting

22 CHARLES ROAD,
LONDON W1.
3rd May 19--

Dear Chester,

Thank you very much for asking me to go to the theatre with you next Thursday. I should love to. Your theatre parties are always such fun and Soyinka is a playwright whose work I particularly admire. And of course I'd enjoy having dinner with you afterwards, and gladly accept your offer of a lift home.

Till Thursday,

Love,

SANDY

132 Declining

22 CHARLES ROAD,
LONDON W1.
3rd May 19--

Dear Chester,

Alas, I already have an engagement on Thursday evening which I fear I cannot break. I am very disappointed, as your theatre parties are always such fun, but I'm sure that you will have no trouble in finding someone to take my place. Thanks, anyway, for asking me.

Love from
SANDY

133   Thanking

22 CHARLES ROAD,
LONDON W1.
12th May 19--

Dear Chester,

    This is just a short note to thank you for a wonderful evening. I thoroughly enjoyed the play and I thought that Jackson's performance was a real tour de force. And what an excellent dinner – I shall not forget that delicious sole in a hurry!

Love from
SANDY

134   Invitation to a Children's Party

21 COWLEY STREET,
LONDON W6.
10th December 19--

Dear Mrs Ahmed,

    Would Tamara be able to come to a children's party at our house on 14th January? It is Lucy's birthday and she is asking most of Form II so there should be lots of Tamara's friends here. The party starts at four and I hope that it will finish by seven.

    Perhaps you would like to come in for a drink when you collect her.

Yours,
MARGARET BRAY

135   Accepting

15 PRATT ROAD,
LONDON NW8.
15th December 19--

Dear Mrs Bray,

    How kind of you to ask Tamara to Lucy's party! She would love to come and is very excited about it. My husband will collect her on his

108

way back from work and I'm sure he would be delighted to look in for a quick drink.

With many thanks,

Yours ever,

SONIA AHMED

136   Declining

15 PRATT ROAD,

LONDON NW8.

15th January 19--

Dear Mrs Bray,

Thank you very much for asking Tamara to Lucy's birthday party. Unfortunately, she is spending the last few days of the holidays with her aunt in Devon, so I'm afraid that she won't be able to come.

Please will you wish Lucy a very happy birthday from us.

Yours ever,

SONIA AHMED

137   Invitation to an Acquaintance to Stay for the Week-end

SEA VIEW,

KINGSBRIDGE,

DEVON.

(postcode)

7th September 19--

Dear Mr Brendon,

If you are free on the week-end of 19th–21st September, we should be very pleased to welcome you here. I do hope that you will be able to come and will send you directions or times of suitable trains to Totnes as soon as I hear from you.

Yours sincerely,

BARBARA PARSONS

138   Accepting

21 Holly Court,
Russell Hill,
London NW2.
12th September 19--

Dear Mrs Parsons

Thank you very much indeed for your kind invitation which I am happy to accept. I am much looking forward to the week-end of the 19th. It is more convenient for me to come by car and I'd be most grateful if you could send me a brief sketchmap of the best route to follow after one leaves the motorway.

Yours sincerely,
Hugh Brendon

139   Declining

21 Holly Court,
Russell Hill,
London NW2.
12th September 19--

Dear Mrs Parsons

How very kind of you to ask me to stay for the week-end! It would have given me the greatest pleasure to be able to accept, but some business colleagues from Canada will be in London that week-end and I have promised to show them the sights.

I do appreciate your kindness in asking me and make so bold as to hope that you will do so again.

Yours sincerely,
Hugh Brendon

140   Thanking

21 Holly Court,
Russell Hill,
London NW2.
28th May 19--

Dear Mrs Parsons,

Very many thanks for a delightful week-end. After a hard week at the office a couple of days in such idyllic surroundings are an ideal tonic, and I returned to the City on Monday feeling both refreshed and relaxed.

I know how seldom you come to London – and who can wonder at your not wanting to leave such a paradise? – but when next you do, I hope that you will let me know and allow me to take you out to lunch or dinner. It would give me great pleasure.

Yours sincerely,

HUGH BRENDON

141   Invitation to a Friend for a Week-end Visit

PERCHWOOD HOUSE,
TUCKENHAY,
TOTNES,
S. DEVON.
(postcode)
29th December 19--

My dear Eileen,

Is there any chance of your coming to stay for the week-end of 16th–18th January? The Warrens, whom you met the last time you were here, are coming to dinner on the Saturday and particularly asked if they could meet you again. I'm sure it would do you a power of good to get away for a couple of nights. Do come!

Much love,

JOAN

142   Accepting

4 ISLINGTON ROAD,
LONDON N3.
2nd January 19--

My dear Joan,

How kind of you to ask me down for the week-end of the 16th! I'd love to come and am longing to see you and Norman again. I am very flattered by what you say about the Warrens and only hope that I shall live up to their expectations!

Much love,

EILEEN

143 Thanking

4 ISLINGTON ROAD,
LONDON N3.
19th January 19--

My dear Joan,

What a delightful week-end! I enjoyed every minute and feel thoroughly reinvigorated after a couple of days of clean country air.

It was great fun to meet the Warrens again. They are so amusing and intelligent, and suit each other so perfectly.

I am sending you, by way of a totally inadequate thankyou present, a copy of the book we were talking about at dinner on Saturday.

Again very many thanks,

With much love,

EILEEN

144 Formal Note to be Sent with a Twenty-first Birthday Present

To Sophie, on the occasion of her twenty-first birthday, with very best wishes from Dr and Mrs Williams.

OR

To Sophie, on the occasion of her twenty-first birthday with best wishes for today and for her future happiness, from John and Sally Williams.

145 To a Friend on her Twenty-first Birthday

12 RIGBY ROAD,
SOUTHAMPTON.
(postcode)
11th September 19--

Dearest Laura,

I hope that this letter will reach you in time to wish you a very, very happy birthday tomorrow. How I wish that I could be there to celebrate the occasion with you, but, as you know, it is just not possible. I'm sure the party will be a great success and long to hear all about it when we meet. Meanwhile I send you my very best wishes for tomorrow and for the future.

With fondest love,

JEAN

146   To a Godchild on his Twenty-first Birthday

BISHOP'S HOUSE,
VOWCHURCH,
HEREFORDSHIRE.
(postcode)
8th May 19--

My dear Peter,

This letter brings you my very best wishes for your twenty-first birthday.

I suppose that, as your godfather, I should offer you some sound advice on this important occasion, but I have no intention of spoiling the day for you by moralizing. If you continue to work as hard and to behave as sensibly as you did at school and at university, I'm sure that you won't need any guidance from me in achieving all the success and happiness which I devoutly wish you.

I enclose a cheque which I expect you to spend in the most self-indulgent manner that your imagination can devise!

Your loving godfather,
HENRY

147   Thanking

CRAVEN COTTAGE,
AMBERLEY,
SUSSEX.
(postcode)
12th May 19--

Dear Uncle Henry,

Thank you very much indeed for your most generous cheque, and for all the kind things which you said in your letter. I hardly feel that I deserve such compliments. I am not going to be over hasty in deciding how to spend the money but I can assure you that your instructions regarding self-indulgence will be strictly adhered to!

I'm so sorry that you could not come to the party. Everyone said that it was a great success.

Again very many thanks,

With love from
PETER

148　Letter Accompanying a Birthday Present

ELECTRONIC HOUSE,
ALLEN ROAD,
LONDON SE22.
4th March 19--

Dear Sally,

This is to wish you a very happy birthday. I am afraid that my inspiration failed me, so I have taken the lazy way out and sent you an azalea. If you look after it, it will flower each year.

Love from
GERALD

149　Thanking

FLAT 4A,
WESTON COURT,
POPES LANE,
LONDON SW7.
6th March 19--

Dear Gerald,

The azalea arrived this morning and is on my table as I write. It is the perfect colour for this room and is certainly not a lazy present. You are very kind and thoughtful and I am most grateful. I only hope that I shall be able to look after it properly; I don't have very green fingers!

Much love,
Sally

150　Letter Accompanying a Birthday Present

47 ASHLEY GARDENS,
SHALFORD, SURREY.
(postcode)
4th November 19--

Dear Michael,

I am afraid that the enclosed book is no surprise as you told me that you wanted to read it, but it comes with my love and best wishes for a very happy birthday. When you have read it, I'd love to know what you think of it.

Much love,

JENNIFER

151   Thanking

RIVER HOUSE,
GREAT SUTTON,
WILTSHIRE.
(postcode)
11th November 19--

My dear Jennifer,

How sweet of you to remember my birthday! The book was indeed a surprise as I had quite forgotten mentioning that I wanted to read it. But you were entirely right, and I am dying to get down to it. As soon as I have read it, I will take you out to dinner and we can have a good talk about it.

I do hope that your new job is going well. You can tell me all about it when we meet.

Love,

MICHAEL

Engagements, Weddings and Births

152   Formal Announcement of an Engagement for Insertion in a Newspaper

Mr G. A. Huntley
and Miss S. C. Richards
The engagement is announced between George, younger son of Mr and Mrs Norman Huntley of Highgate, N6, and Susan, daughter of Mr and Mrs P. G. Richards of Zürich, Switzerland.

153   Informing a Friend of One's Engagement

18 Oakbury Road,
Wargrave,
Berks.
(postcode)
28th May 19--

Dearest Julia,

I am writing to let you know, before the announcement appears in the newspaper on Friday, that Craig and I are engaged to be married. You have always been so good to me that I felt I must let you know myself. My parents are delighted and Mummy is already getting in a flap about the wedding, although we are not planning to get married until October! I'll tell you all about it when we meet.

Much love,
Anthea

154   Acknowledgement

Meadow View,
Lashley's Corner,
Nr. Emsworth,
Hampshire.
(postcode)
30th May 19--

Dearest Anthea,

I was deeply touched that you should have taken the time and trouble to write and tell me that you and Craig are engaged. I need hardly say how thrilled I am for you both. I'm longing to hear all your plans but I can imagine how frantically busy you must be so I won't pester you on the telephone and will try to wait as patiently as I can until I hear from you.

Lots of love,
Julia

155   To a Friend, on her Engagement

CATHEDRAL COTTAGE,
CANTERBURY,
KENT.
(postcode)
1st May 19--

My dearest Lucy,

I have just spoken to your mother on the telephone and she told me that you and Nicholas became officially engaged last night. I tried to ring you to say how absolutely delighted I am for you, but I could get no answer. Nicholas is certainly a very lucky man and I'm sure that you will be blissfully happy together.

I know how terribly busy you must be, so I won't bother you, but if you have a moment to spare do ring me and tell me all your plans.

I can't tell you how happy I am for you.

With fondest love,

KAREN

156   Acknowledgement

47 THE BOLTONS,
MALTON,
YORKS.
(postcode)
7th May 19--

Dearest Karen,

How sweet of you to write so promptly. I am a very lucky girl, and I know it. Whether Nicholas is so lucky remains to be seen! I am staying with Sally for a few nights until the fuss blows over, just popping into the flat to get my post. When things are a bit less hectic, I will give you a ring and you must come and have supper so that I can tell you of our plans for the wedding.

Much love,

LUCY

157 To an Acquaintance, on her Engagement

WOOD FARM HOUSE,
GORHAM,
ST ALBANS.
(postcode)
8th July 19--

Dear Penny,

I have just seen the announcement of your engagement in the paper and would like to send you, on behalf of Mrs Martin and myself, our very best wishes for your future happiness.

Yours sincerely,

TIMOTHY MARTIN

158 Acknowledgement

12 WEST STREET,
LONDON SW7.
20th July 19--

Dear Mr Martin,

Thank you very much for your kind letter. It was thoughtful of you to write. My fiancé will be here next week-end and perhaps I may bring him round to meet you. I am sure you will like him.

Yours sincerely,

PENNY LAWRENCE

159 From a Bride-to-be Asking a Friend to Act as Bridesmaid

STRAITS VIEW,
PAGET STREET,
ANGLESEY,
GWYNEDD.
(postcode)
13th June 19--

Darling Jane,

I am writing on behalf of Henry and myself to ask if you will be a bridesmaid at our wedding. We do hope that you will consent, but Henry thought that it would be better for me to write to you, just in case you would rather not. Henry's two nephews are to be pages (they can't say 'no'!) and we hope that Alice will be the other grown-up bridesmaid.

Fondest love,

SHIRLEY

160 Accepting

95 VALLEY RISE,
BRENTFORD.
(postcode)
15th June 19––

Darling Shirley,

Of course I shall be delighted to be one of your bridesmaids. I am thrilled and flattered that you and Henry should ask me. I am dying to know what we are going to wear but I won't worry you as I know how busy you must be. Let me know about fittings etc. in due course. Many thanks for asking me.

Love,

JANE

161 Declining

95 VALLEY RISE,
BRENTFORD.
(postcode)
15th June 19––

Darling Shirley,

It was kind of you and Henry to ask me to be a bridesmaid at your wedding and I hope that you won't think me terribly rude and ungrateful if I decline, but I do feel quite strongly that a bridesmaid should be younger than the bride. I don't want to sound like a disgruntled old maid and I am very flattered that you should ask me, but honestly my bridesmaid days are over. Forgive me.

Fondest love,

JANE

162   Asking a Friend to Act as Best Man

SEATON CLOSE,
CULLOMPTON,
DEVON.
(postcode)
20th April 19--

My dear Sam,

I write to ask if you will do me the honour of being my best man at the forthcoming turning-point in my life. As you well know, I have no near relative who could suitably undertake the role, and I would rather have you than anyone else. You would give me, who regard you as my oldest and closest friend, very much pleasure by so doing.

Yours ever,
BRUCE

163   Accepting

STONE COTTAGE,
HELSTON, CORNWALL.
(postcode)
28th April 19--

My dear Bruce,

I shall be delighted to act as your best man and I am extremely flattered that you should ask me.

Do you want me to say a few words at the reception? If so, I assure you that they will be very few! I do not approve of best men who try to steal the show by making long speeches peppered with feeble jokes on an occasion which, in my mind, belongs entirely to the bride and bridegroom!

Yours ever,
SAM

164   Declining

STONE COTTAGE,
HELSTON, CORNWALL.
(postcode)
28th April 19--

My dear Bruce,

I am flattered that you should ask me to be your best man and I earnestly hope that our friendship, which I value greatly, will not be in any way affected by my refusal. As you know I have never been able to accept enough of the teachings of the Church to call myself a Christian and therefore I do not think it right that I should play a prominent role in a ceremony of such great significance to you and Janet. I do hope that you will understand and will forgive me.

Yours ever,

SAM

165   Formal Invitation to a Wedding

Mr & Mrs Bernard Jeffreys

Mr and Mrs William Scott
request the pleasure of
your company at the marriage
of their daughter
Clare
to
Mr Alexander Clough
at St Christopher's Church, Booker
on Tuesday 12th January 19--
at 3 o'clock
and afterwards at
The Keswick Arms Hotel

RSVP
   Paterson House,
     Newport,
       Somerset.
         (postcode)

---

63 CRESCENT ROAD,
HAMPSTEAD,
LONDON NW3.
20th November 19--

Mr and Mrs Bernard Jeffreys have much pleasure in accepting the kind invitation of Mr and Mrs William Scott to the wedding of their daughter Clare on 12th January.

167   Formal Announcement of a Marriage for Insertion in a Newspaper

Mr M. Dixon and Miss C. Phillips
The marriage took place on Saturday at St Philomena's church, Bedford Hill, of Mr Matthew Dixon, son of Mr and Mrs B.O. Dixon of Clapham, and Miss Cynthia Phillips, daughter of Mr and Mrs R. A. Phillips, of Battersea Rise. The Rev. Alan Peel officiated. Mr Barry Cornish was best man. A reception was held in Balham Town Hall and the honeymoon is being spent in Malta.

168   Formal Announcement of the Birth of a Child for Insertion in a Newspaper

CLIFF – On 12 January 1983 at St Saviour's Hospital, Nairobi, to Nadia (*née* Paget) and Henry – a son.

169   Letter Announcing the Birth of a Child

99 FRIARS AVENUE,
WESTBURY.
(postcode)
17th April 19--

Dear Derek,

I am delighted to tell you that Wendy had a son on Monday night at St Teresa's. Mother and child are doing well. Indeed Wendy is in radiant form and would love to see you. She comes home on Thursday, so why don't you look in for a drink over the week-end?

Yours ever,

TOM

170   Acknowledgement

HOLMWOOD,
WESTBURY.
(postcode)
19th April 19--

Dear Tom,

I was delighted to hear your good news. Please give Wendy my love and congratulations. If it suits you, may I look in at about 12 o'clock on Saturday and pay my respects to your son and heir?

Yours ever,

Derek

171   To an Acquaintance on the Birth of a Child

THE BUNGALOW,
SIDMOUTH.
(postcode)
18th June 19--

Dear Mrs Warren,

My husband has just seen in the paper that you now have a son and joins in me in sending our warmest congratulations and good wishes. I hope that all is going well with you and the baby.

Yours sincerely,

JOAN M. CLIFF

172   To a Friend on the Birth of a Child

178 BEDFORD HILL,
BRISTOL.
(postcode)
9th April 19--

Dearest Cynthia,

We were thrilled to hear your splendid news and send you our love and congratulations. Matthew must be as proud as a peacock now that he has a son and heir. Kevin can't get away from the shop for the next couple of days but we are planning to come and see you on Saturday. I'm sure that Matthew has catered for your every need, but if there is *anything* you want, do let us know.

Longing to see you and the baby,

Fondest love,

PAT

173 Thanking a Friend for Flowers Sent on the Birth of a Child

481 BOURNE AVENUE,
BIRMINGHAM.
(postcode)
20th April 19--

Dear Jane,

How very sweet of you and Martin to send me such beautiful flowers! Thank you both very much indeed. I am coming home on Wednesday and I hope that you will both visit me and meet Adam. So far he seems a very peaceful baby, but I've no doubt he'll soon learn to use his lungs.

With love,

TESSA

174 To a Friend, Asking him to be a Godfather

PARKWAY,
SLAPTON, DEVON.
(postcode)
5th May 19--

Dear Ronnie,

I am writing to ask you if you would be prepared to be one of Henry's godfathers. I realize that it is a rather backhanded compliment involving a certain amount of trouble and expense over the years, and that is why I am asking you by letter. If you would rather not you can more easily refuse, but as Brenda and I regard you as one of our very closest friends, we naturally hope that you will agree to do so.

Yours ever,

KEITH

175 Accepting

41 Broad Street,
Hove, Sussex.
(postcode)
7th May 19--

Dear Keith,

   I am extremely flattered that you and Brenda should ask me to be one of Henry's godfathers, a position which I accept with pride and humility, and which I shall do my best to fulfil conscientiously.

Yours ever,

RONNIE

176 Declining

41 Broad Street,
Hove, Sussex.
(postcode)
7th May 19--

Dear Keith,

   I am very flattered that you and Brenda should ask me to be one of Henry's godfathers and hope that you won't think it ungracious if I decline, but I really don't think that I would make a very suitable godparent. As you know my work obliges me to travel continuously and I do feel that the ideal godparent should be someone with a more settled way of life than my own. I hope you will forgive me.

Yours ever,

RONNIE

177 To a Vicar Asking him to Baptise a Child

20 Surrey Lane,
Bradford, Yorkshire.
(postcode)
22nd April 19--

Dear Mr Gregory,

   I write to ask you whether you would be prepared to baptise our son Angus, who is now two months old. Although my wife and I were both brought up as regular churchgoers, I must confess that latterly our attendance has been sporadic. We were married two years ago at St Mungo's, Skipton, near the home of my wife's parents and have lived here for the past eighteen months. It is certainly our intention that Angus should be brought up as a regular churchgoer.

Yours sincerely,

ALISON SMITH

Illness and Death

178 To an Invalid in Hospital

4 WHITEWING LANE,
DEAL.
(postcode)
9th March 19--

Dear Pauline,

I was upset to hear that you have had to go back into hospital. I rang the sister this morning who said that you were making good progress and would be out in a few days, which is certainly excellent news. Nevertheless, it is very tiresome for you and you have all my sympathy. I wish I could come and see you but, alas, time and distance make it impossible, so I have sent you a few paperbacks which I hope will help to pass the time.

Much love,

LOUISE

179 Acknowledgement

WARD 4B,
ST BRIDE'S HOSPITAL,
LONDON SW18.
12th March 19--

Dear Louise,

Many thanks for your sweet letter and for the parcel of paperbacks, which, I can see, were chosen with great care. They will help enormously to relieve the monotony.

I am happy to say that I am responding well to treatment and the doctor is very pleased with my progress. He says that, if all goes well, I can go home at the end of the week.

Again, many thanks for the books.

Much love,

PAULINE

180   To a Young Acquaintance in Hospital

4 GORDON PLACE,
BATH.
(postcode)
8th August 19--

Dear Peter,

I am very sorry to hear that you have been taken into hospital and are to have an operation. However, it is not a very serious affair these days and you will feel much better when it has been done. My wife asks me to say that if there is anything she can do, you have only to let her know. Please don't be shy about ringing up if we can help in any way.

Yours,

DAVID HODGSON

181   Acknowledgement

PITMAN WARD,
ST ANTHONY'S HOSPITAL,
BATH.
(postcode)
14th August 19--

Dear Mr Hodgson,

I really appreciated your kindness in taking the trouble to write to me. Please will you thank your wife very much indeed for her generous offer, but, in fact, I need nothing. I am happy to say that the operation was quite straight-forward and I am being allowed out in a couple of days. Nevertheless I'm very grateful to you for your concern.

Yours sincerely,

PETER WALKER

182   To an Older Acquaintance in Hospital

CLAYMORE COTTAGE,
HEMYOCK,
KENT.
(postcode)
7th January 19--

Dear Mr Walker,

I was extremely sorry to hear of your unfortunate accident and send you my profound sympathy. I do hope that you are not in too much discomfort and will soon be on your feet again.

Yours sincerely,

DAVID HODGSON

183   Acknowledgement

DRUMMOND WARD,
THE COTTAGE HOSPITAL,
HEMYOCK,
KENT.
(postcode)
10th January 19--

Dear David,

How very kind of you to write to me. It certainly cheers one up to feel that one is not forgotten! I'm glad to be able to tell you that my bones have been successfully glued together again and, come the spring, I should be ready to take a set off you at the Club!

Yours,

PETER WALKER

184   To a Young Woman, Informing her of her Mother's Illness

75 BEECH AVENUE,
LONDON SW15.
25th November 19--

Dear Caroline,

As I have no way of reaching you by telephone, I am sending this letter by first-class post to tell you that your mother has been in bed for the last three days with bronchitis. She asked me not to worry you but as she has not so far responded to the antibiotics which the doctor prescribed, I decided to take it upon myself to let you know. It was most fortunate that I was staying with her when she was taken ill, and I am quite happy to stay on until she is well enough to look after herself. The doctor is coming again today so if you can ring me when you get this letter, I will let you know how she is and what the doctor said.

Yours,
With love,
JANE DRINKWATER

185   Announcement of a Death for Insertion in a Newspaper

JAKES – On 25th January 1983, after a short illness, Timothy Jakes, husband of Catherine Jakes, of Hampstead Villas, Beckenham. Funeral, Monday 31st January at 12 noon, Bromley Cemetery.

186   To a Close Friend, on the Death of his Wife

SHAMROCK COTTAGE,
EYE,
SUFFOLK.
(postcode)
4th February 19--

Dear Simon,

I realize how vain must be these or any other words to ease your sorrow but I do want you to know that the love and sympathy of Glenda and myself are very much with you. Fate has dealt you a bitter blow and time alone will help you to smile on fate and meet it on equal terms. For the present I hope that you will allow us to help in all and every way we can.

Your loving friends,
GLENDA AND ANTHONY

187 Acknowledgement

5 PARKWAY,
EYE,
SUFFOLK.
(postcode)
10th February 19--

Dear Anthony,

It was kind of you and Glenda to write and I hasten to take you up on your offer. Mary's funeral, as you know, is on Wednesday at 3 o'clock and I wonder if I could come back with you after the service and stay for two or three nights. I have been so busy these last few days that I have hardly had time to realize what has happened – but I don't think I could bear to come back here straight from the funeral. I'll try not to be too much of a wet blanket!

Yours ever,
SIMON

188 To an Acquaintance, on the Death of his Wife

FAIRWAYS,
BAGSHOT,
SURREY.
(postcode)
6th July 19--

Dear Peter,

It was with great sadness that I read in the paper the tragic news of Barbara's death. Alice joins me in sending you our sincerest condolences. If we can be of help in any way at all, don't hesitate to let me know.

Yours,
JIM

189 Acknowledgement

44 PRINCES LANE,
ACTON,
LONDON W3.
10th July 19--

Dear Jim,

Very many thanks for your kind letter and offer of help. I am managing to cope fairly well in the circumstances, but it is a great comfort to know that one has such kind and caring friends and colleagues.

Yours,

PETER

190 To a Young Lady, Condoling with her on the Death of her Mother

1 NORTON CLOSE,
CANTERBURY,
KENT.
(postcode)
2nd January 19--

My dear Jane,

It was with great sadness that I read of your mother's death. I know how deeply you will miss her but at least you have the comfort of knowing that she had had a long and happy life and that you were able to care for her during her last illness. No mother could have wished for a better daughter.

Do let me know if there is anything I can do.

Yours affectionately,

MARGARET HERRING

191 To the Wife of a Business Acquaintance on her Husband's Death

HILLVIEW,
PRESTEIGNE,
POWYS.
(postcode)
10th January 19--

Dear Mrs Stone,

It was with great regret that I learned today of the death of your husband. As you know we worked together for some years and few were in a better position than I to recognize his many fine qualities. I send you my deepest sympathy.

Yours sincerely,

LLOYD WATKINS

131

192   Letter of Condolence on the Death of a Child

ROMAN WALK,
BATH,
AVON.
(postcode)
14th February 19--

Dearest Jane,

Robert and I have just heard the tragic news and send you and Peter our deepest sympathy. Words are of no avail at such a time, but we want you to know that you are very much in our thoughts and Sarah in our prayers.

With fondest love,

ANGELA

193   Acknowledgement

3 BLACKBERRY LANE,
WINSLEY,
WILTSHIRE.
(postcode)
20th February 19--

Dearest Angela,

Very many thanks for your kind letter. Sarah's death has been a terrible blow to us and life seems totally empty and pointless without her, but it is a great comfort to know that one has the love and sympathy of one's friends.

With much love,

JANE

194   Announcing a Death to an Acquaintance

18B EATON TERRACE,
BRENTWOOD,
ESSEX.
(postcode)
13th November 19--

Dear Mrs Bensah,

As I know that you were away on holiday last week, I don't expect that you have heard the sad news of my father's death. He was ill for only two days and died peacefully in his sleep, so one must at least be grateful that he suffered very little at the end. Please do not bother to acknowledge this letter.

Yours sincerely,

KOFI EGALA

195   To a Relative, Asking him to Attend a Funeral

14 GRAND AVENUE,
LONDON NW8.
16th April 19--

Dear Uncle James,

I write, as promised when we spoke on the telephone, to let you have the details of Mother's funeral. It is to be at 12 noon next Wednesday (21st) at Willesden Cemetery. Dad is still very shocked and bewildered so I particularly hope that you will be able to come, in order to give him a bit of support.

With love from

VERA

196   To an Uncle Abroad Announcing the Death of a Parent

71A WATFORD WAY,
LONDON N19.
14th February 19--

Dear Uncle Gopichand,

You will, I know, be very sad to hear that Father died suddenly last week. He had been at work all day, complained of a pain in his chest when he came home and went to his room to lie down. When Mother went in to see him 30 minutes later he was dead. He had had a heart attack. At least the end was painless. Mother, as you would expect, has taken the blow very well but inwardly is obviously suffering a lot. I am glad that you were able to visit us last summer and see them so happy together, and I know how much it would mean to Mother if you were able to come over again this year.

Your loving

INDIRA

133

197   From a Lady to her Brother-in-law, Informing him of the Death of her Husband

71 PENFOLD ROAD,
ESHER,
SURREY.
(postcode)
7th May 19--

My dear Darren,

    You will have received my telegram telling you that Wayne was sinking fast. He died in his sleep last night and I don't think that he suffered at all, for which one must be thankful. It would be a great relief to me if you could come and help with the arrangements. There is so much to be done and at the moment I find it impossible to concentrate on anything for long.

With love,
MARILYN

Life Assurance

Note **Whole Life Policy** is a contract on a person whose life is assured, under which policy money is paid at death.

Endowment Policy is one in which money is paid at maturity or death, whichever occurs first.

Joint Life Policy is on the lives of two persons, and money is usually payable to the survivor on the death of the other.

Surrender Value is the amount paid by the insurers in consideration for the cancellation of a policy.

Loan Value is the amount of money you can borrow on your policy, normally becomes 90% of the Surrender Value.

Capital Transfer Tax. This tax has replaced Estate Duty and makes tax payable only on the death of a husband or wife, whichever is the later.

198   To an Assurance Company, Regarding Monthly Premiums on a Whole Life Policy

21 VALIANT HOUSE,
MADDEN CRESCENT,
LONDON SW11.
24th August 19--

Dear Sirs,

Re: Whole Life and Endowment Policies

I am interested in taking out a Whole Life Policy and my wife an Endowment Policy, premiums to be payable on a monthly basis. My age will be 29 next birthday and my wife will be 26.

I would like to invest £20.00 per month (gross) and would be grateful for a quotation based on this amount for both a Whole Life With and Without Profits Policy.

My wife wishes to invest £10.00 per month (gross) on a 30 year Endowment and would like a quotation on a With and Without Profit basis, both to show your estimated surrender values after 15 and 20 years.

Yours faithfully,

PETER BENNETT

199   Asking for Whole Life Assurance Rates

18 OAKBURY ROAD,
BRETHERTON,
LANCS.
(postcode)
4th June 19--

Dear Sirs,

Please send me your prospectus together with specific quotations for the following:

Whole Life Assurance, With Profits for a female life born 28th August 19--.

Whole Life Assurance, Without Profits in the case of a male life born 23rd July 19--.

In both cases the quotations should be based on an annual premium of £200.00.

Yours faithfully,

BELINDA COURTAULD (MRS)

200 Asking for a Last Survivor Annuity

HARBOUR COTTAGE,
HAMBLEDON,
HAMPSHIRE
(postcode)
16th May 19--

Dear Sirs,

Please send me details of your annual premium for an annuity of £4000 a year to commence in ten years' time, this to continue until the death of one of two lives – a lady born 22.5.19-- and a gentleman born 12.3.19--, the annuity to continue to the last survivor at one-half the original amount, ie £2000 p.a.

Yours faithfully,
HUBERT DUTTON

201 Asking for a Joint Life Assurance

3 RIVER VIEW,
LONDON SW3,
14th January 19--

Dear Sirs,

Would you kindly let me have your quotation for a Life Assurance for £10,000, payable on the death of a lady aged 40 last birthday or of a gentleman aged 41 last birthday, whichever should happen first. I should like the policy to be a With Profits one.

Please do not send a representative until I ask that one should call.

Yours faithfully,
MICHAEL BRYAN

202 Regarding Assurances for One's Son

7 LIFEBOAT WALK,
BEMBRIDGE,
ISLE OF WIGHT.
(postcode)
1st February 19--

Dear Sirs,

Would you please let me have details of policies in respect of a child born on 30th December 19--.

1   Whole Life Assurance, With and Without Profits, with the option of changing to some form of Endowment Assurance at age 18, the premiums to be paid by me, the father, up to that time or up to my death should that occur previously.

2   The same as 1, but premiums not ceasing should my death occur before my son's attaining age 18.

3   A School Fees Plan, the sum assured under which could be taken up at specific periods of the child's life – say £1200 per annum for six years commencing at age 10 and £1800 per annum for four years from age 16.

4   Any other suggestions that you may have to make.

I believe that by taking out a policy before the child attains three months, I should pay a lower rate of premium. Is this so?

My age is 30 last birthday and I am prepared to invest in the region of £1000 per annum.

Yours faithfully,

NICHOLAS SAMPSON

203   Asking for Annuity Rates

105 RADNOR WALK,

HORNBY,

LANCS.

(postcode)

2nd May 19--

Dear Sirs,

Would you kindly let me know, at your earliest convenience, the amount of Immediate Annuity that can be obtained for purchase money of £5000, in the case of a male 63 next birthday, ie on 4.9.19--. Would you also show the figures were you to build in a 3% annual increase to the annuity.

It would be preferable if the annuity could be made payable by quarterly instalments.

Yours faithfully,

PETER KEMP

204   Asking for a Short-term Life Assurance

61 ARTHUR ROAD,
TUNBRIDGE WELLS,
KENT.
(postcode)
6th May 19--

Dear Sirs,

I am making a six-month business trip to South Africa commencing on the 1st September next and wish to know your rate of premium for Life Assurance cover during this period.

I would like the basic cover to be £50,000, with double this amount to be payable in the event of my dying through an accident.

Air travel will certainly be involved while I am in South Africa as well as journeys out and back, but all flights will be with recognized air lines.

My occupation is that of Sales Director for a mining equipment manufacturing company and the premium would be paid by them.

May I also have details for medical cover, baggage insurance etc.

Yours faithfully,

ANDREW PRIDEAUX

205   Inquiring about the Surrender Value of a Policy

WHITBOURNE FARM,
CORSLEY,
WILTSHIRE.
(postcode)
19th September 19--

Dear Sirs,

Re: Policy No. -------

Will you please let me know the Surrender Value of the above policy. I should also like to know the maximum amount I could take as a loan on this policy should I decide not to surrender it. Would I have to pay interest if I took the loan? If so, at what rate?

Yours faithfully,

SUSAN PHILLIPS

OLD BURSLEDON,
SOUTHAMPTON,
HAMPSHIRE.
(postcode)
9th January 19--

Dear Sirs,

I have an estate valued at some £150,000. My son tells me that I can invest up to £2000 per annum as a premium on a Life Assurance Policy, this to be on my life for his absolute benefit; this divestment would not, I understand, break the rules concerning disposals of my Estate in any one year.

He further tells me that the resultant proceeds of the policy would be free of both ordinary tax and Capital Tax. Is this correct?

I would be most grateful to know the amount of Capital Transfer Tax that would be payable by my son on my death. I am a widower and he is my sole beneficiary.

I will be 64 next birthday and have a mild heart condition. Would this present a problem in purchasing Life Assurance to minimize my son's ultimate Capital Transfer Tax obligations?

Yours faithfully,
NEIL DRYSDALE

207   Regarding Assurance and House Purchase

174 LONG LANE,
WINDSOR,
BERKS.
(postcode)
19th June 19--

The ----- Assurance Company Ltd

Dear Sirs,

I am considering the purchase of a house at Rhos, Anglesey and have approached the ----- Building Society concerning a loan. They have agreed to let me have a mortgage of £15,000, being 80% of the purchase price, repayable over 20 years. They have referred me to you for details of an Endowment Policy. The sum assured on £15,000 would pay off the Mortgage were I to die prior to the end of the 20-year repayment period and thus leave my wife and children with a debt-free house.

Would you please give me full details.

I was 40 on the 12th October and am in excellent health, but I should be quite happy to undergo a medical examination with your Company.

Yours faithfully,

MARK SAVAGE

208 Asking for the Premium of a Life Policy to be Paid out of its Surrender Value

244 HESKETH ROAD,
SOUTHEND,
ESSEX.
(postcode)
15th October 19--

Dear Sirs,

Re: Policy No. -----

I have received your notice that the premium on the above Life Policy is due. I am currently unemployed and I shall be obliged therefore if you will pay this premium out of the surrender value, in accordance with the terms of the policy. I hope to repay the amount when my situation improves.

Yours faithfully,

CHARLES WISE

209 Claiming Payment under a Life Policy
(with reference to the Married Woman's Property Act Provision)

124 HAZEL AVENUE,
BISHOPSTONE,
DERBYSHIRE.
(postcode)
18th February 19--

Dear Sirs,

Re: Policy No: ---------.

I have to inform you that my husband Robert Beaumont died on Friday last. I am appointed sole executor and legatee by his Will.

I enclose the Death Certificate and, as Policy No.----- was written under the MWPA, I would be grateful if the proceeds from this policy could be forwarded immediately. I will lodge with you the probate as soon as it is received, when I hope you will let me have a prompt settlement of Policy No. ------.

Yours faithfully,

EMMA BEAUMONT

Letters to Banks and Accountants

210   Asking for a Loan Account

15 CHURCH ROAD,
CHRISTCHURCH,
DORSET.
19th July 19--

a/c No. ....

The Manager,

.... Bank

Dear Sir,

I am having some difficulty in controlling my expenditure and you will know that my current account becomes overdrawn from time to time, without prior arrangement.

It occurs to me that the best way of dealing with the matter would be for me to have a loan account of, say, £500 with transfers of £20 per month which I can afford from current account by way of repayment. This should enable me to keep my current account in credit on a permanent basis.

Please let me know if you consider this is a sensible solution. I feel sure it will be much tidier and help us both to know better where we stand.

Yours faithfully,

JAMES METCALFE

211 Request for a Bridging Loan

19 STAFFORD ROAD,
ALDWORTH,
BERKSHIRE.
9th April 19--

a/c No. . . . . . .

The Manager,

. . . . Bank

Dear Sir,

Following my retirement, my wife and I have decided to move to Bridgwater and have found a suitable property at a cost of £35,000. Our present home is up for sale at a figure of £47,950 and one or two people have expressed interest, but a firm sale has not yet been agreed.

The vendors in Bridgwater are pressing for me to sign a contract and I should like to do so, but I may have to complete for the new property before I have sold my existing one.

Would it be possible to have a Bridging Loan until my house is sold for, say, a period of six months? The Deeds of my present house are free of mortgage and I can deposit them with you by way of security.

If you require further details, I shall be happy to come and see you.

Yours faithfully,

B. S. FORD

212 Asking for Information about a Business Development Loan

POLE COTTAGE,
BINGHAM,
NOTTINGHAMSHIRE.
(postcode)
21st May 19--

a/c No. . . . .

The Manager,

. . . . Bank

Dear Sir,

I have taken the option of retiring early and under the terms of the scheme offered by my employer I have received the sum of £10,000 in cash. I shall be paid a slightly reduced pension from that payable had I worked to normal retirement age.

142

I am now looking for something to occupy my time and am considering setting up a small business. A village store and post office in my locality is up for sale at a cost of £20,000 including the remainder of the lease, fixtures and fittings, stock and goodwill.

I believe it is possible to have a Business Development Loan over say a 10-year period to enable me to complete the purchase. I should be prepared to put £8000 into the purchase and would ask you to consider lending me the remainder.

There are no doubt more details you will require and if it is convenient I would like to call on you next Thursday, 27th May, to discuss the proposal, bringing with me Audited Accounts for the business for the last three years. Perhaps you would kindly telephone me to let me know what time would be convenient.

Yours faithfully,

J. S. WEST

213 Another Request for a Loan

17 SUBURBAN WAY,

PURLEY,

SURREY.

(postcode)

2nd May 19--

a/c No. . . . .

The Manager,

. . . . Bank

Dear Sir,

I wish to purchase a caravan for holiday purposes costing £2000. I have £500 in cash available towards the cost and would like to borrow the remainder on a personal loan over two years. I can make the repayments quite comfortably from salary and bonuses over that period.

Will you please send me a form for completion, letting me know in due course whether you are able to grant this facility. I hope to make the purchase in two weeks' time.

Yours faithfully,

TIMOTHY CLARKE

214   Asking for a Temporary Overdraft

197 LACE LANE,
NOTTINGHAM.
(postcode)
1st February 19--

a/c No. . . . .

The Manager,
. . . . Bank

Dear Sir,

I am faced at the moment with one or two items of unexpected expenditure totalling £300 and I should be grateful for an overdraft limit for that amount for a period of three months. My annual bonus will be due at that time and this will restore my account to credit.

Would you please confirm that I may overdraw my account up to £300 in case of need until the 31st August.

Yours faithfully,
E. J. LEWIS

215   Opening a Deposit Account

193 TYNE ROAD,
NEWCASTLE UPON TYNE.
(postcode)
15th May 19--

a/c No. . . . .

The Manager,
. . . . Bank

Dear Sir,

I appear to be building up a surplus of money on my current account which is not earning interest. I should be obliged, therefore, if you would open a deposit account in my name, transferring the sum of £500 from my current account. Would you also please set up a regular standing order to transfer £20 on the 18th of each month until further notice from current account to deposit account. Please send me a statement of the deposit account each quarter.

Yours faithfully,
G.W.R. BIGGS

216   Opening a Second Account

14 ACACIA DRIVE,
NEW MALDEN,
SURREY.
(postcode)
9th December 19--

The Manager,

.... Bank

Dear Sir,

    I enclose a cheque for £250 to be credited to a new account in my name earmarked No. 2 account. Please send me a paying-in book together with a book of 50 crossed cheques for use with the new account and arrange for a statement to be sent with that of my ordinary current account on the 11th of each month.

Yours faithfully,

LORRAINE HIBBERT (MISS)

217   Opening an Account for a Student

OLD BURSLEDON HOUSE,
OLD BURSLEDON,
HAMPSHIRE.
(postcode)
19th September 19--

a/c No. ....

The Manager,

.... Bank

Dear Sir,

    My son is going up to University in October and I should be obliged if you would open an account for him at Warwick Branch for the receipt of his grant cheque.

    If you make the necessary arrangements at your Warwick Branch, I will ask John to call in with his grant cheque during the early part of October to make himself known and to collect his cheque book, paying-in book etc. A specimen of his signature is given below.

    Thanking you for your help.

Yours faithfully,

JACK DRINKWATER

Specimen signature of John Drinkwater ....

218   Request for a Budget Account

WOODLANDS,
NEWBURY,
BERKSHIRE.
(postcode)
19th August 19--

a/c No. . . . .

The Manager,

. . . . Bank

Dear Sir,

As you will know, I have been overdrawing my current account regularly at the end of each month in anticipation of my salary credit and there are one or two large household bills due to be paid. It occurs to me that a Budget Account would be useful so that I can regulate my expenditure more evenly over a twelve-month period.

Would you, therefore, please send me the necessary forms for completion so that I may open a Budget Account, and let me have an indication of the charges involved.

Yours faithfully,
MARK DENNIS

219   Request for a Joint Account

LUNA COTTAGE,
ABERFELDY,
TAYSIDE.
(postcode)
14th February 19--

a/c No. . . . .

The Manager,

. . . . Bank

Dear Sir,

I write to inform you that I was married on the 2nd February and should be obliged if you would add the name of my wife to the account at present in my sole name. A copy of the marriage certificate is enclosed which please return. No doubt you will send me a form of mandate for completion covering future operations on the account. My wife will require a cheque book and a paying-in book. Please note that the address to which all future correspondence should be sent is that shown at the top of this letter. I enclose a specimen of my wife's signature.

Yours faithfully,

C. F. HAYNES

220　Asking for a Monthly Statement

15 HART STREET,
BURFORD,
GLOUCESTERSHIRE.
(postcode)
12th February 19--

a/c No. . . . .

The Manager,

. . . . Bank

Dear Sir,

At the moment you send me a statement each half year, but I am finding this too infrequent to enable me to keep a proper check on my account. Would you, therefore, in future kindly send me a statement on the 25th of each month.

Yours faithfully,

ROBIN DUTTON

221　Stopping Payment of a Cheque

15 RIVER WALK,
LIMEHOUSE,
LONDON E1.
14th May 19--

a/c No. . . . .

The Manager,

. . . . Bank

Dear Sir,

I write to confirm my telephoned request of today asking you to stop payment of cheque number 23849 dated . . . . drawn for £560 in favour of John P. Loomis and Co. A replacement cheque has been issued and I will advise you if the original one comes to hand so that you may cancel this instruction.

Yours faithfully,

R. GREGORY

222   Request for a Cash Card

15 Lego Lane,
Corsley,
Wilts.
(postcode)
25th April 19--

a/c No. . . . .

The Manager,

. . . . Bank

Dear Sir,

I should find it convenient to have a card for use in your Cash Dispensing machines. If I could draw up to £100 in cash by this method, in any one week, it should be sufficient for my requirements.

Yours faithfully,

J. Steiner

223   Request for a Cheque Card

Hursell Cottage,
Oakham,
Kent.
(postcode)
22nd March 19--

a/c No. . . . .

The Manager,

. . . . Bank

Dear Sir,

I should like to have a Credit Card. Would you please send the necessary application form for completion.

Yours faithfully,

J. M. Bailey

224   Request for Travellers' Cheques

73 WOODVILLE ROAD,
OXFORD.
(postcode)
19th February 19--

a/c No. . . . .

The Manager,

. . . . Bank

Dear Sir,

    My wife and I are going to America on holiday next month and will require some travellers' cheques and currency. We shall be in town on Thursday, 28th July. Would you please have ready for us to collect £500 in travellers' cheques and £100 worth of US notes in, say $10 bills.

    I am uncertain at the moment from an exchange rate point of view whether it is preferable to take travel cheques expressed in US$ or sterling and I suggest that you supply whichever you think best. Please take this letter as your authority to debit our account with the cost of the travel facilities and any expenses involved.

Yours faithfully,

L. J. PATTERSON

225   Request for a Standing Order

5 REGENCY VALE,
BRIGHTON,
SUSSEX.
(postcode)
21st February 19--

a/c No. . . . .

The Manager,

. . . . Bank

Dear Sir,

    Commencing on the 25th of this month and on a similar date on each subsequent month, until further notice, will you please pay the sum of £50 to the account of my daughter, Miss B. M. Wells, at . . . . Bank, 41 High Street, Chipping Sodbury. Her account number is . . . . These payments are to be made to the debit of my account number. . . . .

Yours faithfully,

ANDREW WELLS

226   Cancelling a Standing Order

10 GREEN DRIVE,
COWLISHAW,
SURREY.
(postcode)
27th December 19--

a/c No. . . . .

The Manager,

. . . . Bank

Dear Sir,

Would you please cancel immediately my annual standing order to the Nicholson Golf Club as I have resigned my membership.

Yours faithfully,

JAMES WHITAKER

227   Changing a Standing Order

6 OLD HOUSE LANE,
KINGTON,
HEREFORDSHIRE.
(postcode)
2nd May 19--

a/c No. . . . .

The Manager,

. . . . Bank

Dear Sir,

You make regular payments on my behalf on the 23rd of each month to the account in my wife's name at your Branch. Will you please increase the amount of the payment to £175 each month commencing on the 23rd of this month.

Yours faithfully,

TOM LLEWELLYN

228   Asking for Advice about a Will

The Glebe House,
Oadby,
Leicestershire.
(postcode)
21st March 19--

a/c No. . . . .

The Manager,

. . . . Bank

Dear Sir,

I am about to make a Will, but before I instruct my Solicitor to draw up the necessary papers, I should like some advice as to the most beneficial way in which I can arrange my Estate. Would you please, therefore, make an appointment for me to see your Trustee Manager so that I can talk matters over with him. Perhaps you could telephone me with one or two suitable dates.

Yours faithfully,

W. Appleyard

229   Advising of the Death of a Husband

15 Green Lanes,
Gillingham,
Kent.
(postcode)
21st February 19--

a/c No. . . . .

The Manager,

. . . . Bank

Dear Sir,

I write to advise you that my husband died on Wednesday last, the 18th February. As far as the Bank is concerned there is only the joint account in our name. I am, therefore, enclosing a copy of the Death Certificate so that this can be registered in your books and the account can be operated in future in my sole name. Would you please send me a new cheque book and paying-in book.

As you may know, my late husband appointed the family Solicitor, H. T. Jennings, as his Executor and he is dealing with the Estate.

Yours faithfully,

Mavis O'Brien

230 Request for Advice Following the Death of a Wife

97 NORTHERN DRIVE,
SOLIHULL,
WEST MIDLANDS.
(postcode)

a/c No. . . . .   *9th September 19--*

The Manager,
. . . . Bank

Dear Sir,

I have to inform you that my wife died on Thursday last and I am trying to deal with her financial affairs.

As you know, she had a number of investments in her own name and I believe you are holding the various Share Certificates, Bonds, etc. My late wife has accounts with several Building Societies and our holiday home in France is registered in her name. She was a beneficiary under a Trust Fund set up by her father but I am not sure what action I should take regarding this. Unfortunately, she did not leave a Will, and apart from the fact that there are considerable demands on my time at the moment, I am uncertain how to deal with some aspects of her affairs. I think it would be advisable to obtain the help of your Trustee Department to act as Administrators of her Estate. Would you please let me know what needs to be done to arrange this. In the meantime I am enclosing a copy of the Death Certificate for registration in your books. Please return this to me in due course.

Yours faithfully,

R. S. WARREN

231 Giving Instructions Regarding Investments

THE OAST HOUSE,
CHISLEHURST, KENT.
(postcode)

a/c No. . . . .   *9th January 19--*

The Manager,
. . . . Bank

Dear Sir,

You hold my stocks and shares in safe custody and I shall be obliged if you will kindly sell 1000 ICI Ordinary Shares At Best, crediting my

152

current account with the proceeds. Will you please purchase 500 National Westminster Bank Shares At Best, debiting my account with the cost and placing the Share Certificate when received with the remainder of my stocks and shares in safe custody. Please send me a form of mandate for completion so that the dividends from the new purchase can be credited direct to my account.

Yours faithfully,

V. BENNETT

232 Enclosing a Share Certificate for Safe Keeping and Asking for a List of Certificates Held

THE COTTAGE,
PRESTEIGNE,
POWYS.
(postcode)
5th June 19--

a/c No. . . . .

The Manager,

. . . . Bank

Dear Sir,

I enclose three Share Certificates and a life policy which I should be obliged if you would place with the rest of my securities in safe custody.

There have been a number of changes in my investments recently and it would be helpful if you could send me an up-to-date list of the items you are holding on my behalf.

Yours faithfully,

FRANCIS WHITE

233 Request for Advice on Investments

PARK STREAM COTTAGE,
WEST LAVINGTON,
WILTSHIRE.
(postcode)
9th June 19--

a/c No. . . . .

The Manager,

. . . . Bank

Dear Sir,

My investments have not been reviewed for some time and I should like to seek your help in this matter. As you know, I am now retired and need to maximize my income from these investments. I am paying income tax at the standard rate on my pension of £6000 per year and apart from my investments I have no other source of income. Would you please ask your brokers to review my portfolio letting me have a report on their suggestions and recommendations in due course.

Yours faithfully,

Maurice Osborne

234   Request for a Certificate of Interest

Haystacks,

Stoke,

Hampshire.

(postcode)

19th May 19--

a/c No. . . . .

The Manager,

. . . . Bank

Dear Sir,

I have been asked by the Inspector of Taxes to submit a Return of income etc. Would you please send me a Certificate of Interest paid to the Bank during the year ended 5th April last on the loan supplied to me for the extension of my house.

Yours faithfully,

K. L. King

235   Asking for Advice about Income Tax

15 Streatley Road,

Streatham,

London SW12.

4th June 19--

a/c No. . . . .

The Manager,

. . . . Bank

Dear Sir,

My Company has asked me to work in Ghana for two years on a contract which they have secured there.

It will be necessary for me to make various arrangements regarding my salary and the receipt of the rent on my house which I have let. I am

154

not sure how I stand regarding income tax and I would find it helpful to discuss all these matters with you and perhaps an expert from your Income Tax Department. I am free to come to your office at any time which is convenient to you and I should be glad if you would arrange a necessary meeting so that I can put into effect the various arrangements.

Yours faithfully,

C. C. Sykes

236　To an Accountant Giving Details for Income Tax Return

19B Park Way,
Sutton,
Surrey.
(postcode)
30th April 19--

Dear Mr Foster,

I enclose the Income Tax Return for 1981/82 which the Inland Revenue has sent me together with the following which you will need for its preparation.

1　Form P60 for 1982/83 in respect of my earnings from employment.

2　Royalty statements in respect of my literary earnings for 1982/83 together with relevant vouchers for expenses necessarily incurred therein.

3　Dividend Vouchers for 1982/83.

4　Contract notes for purchases and sales of investments. Please contact my stockbrokers if you have any queries about the cost of investments sold in the year.

5　Forms SEPC in respect of retirement annuity premiums paid in the year. I will be taking out a further contract with Pontefract Life Assurance Company in the sum of £500 p.a.

6　Bank deposit interest received from Barclays was: June 1982 – £98.43 and December 1982 – £61.28.

7　Interest received from Scunthorpe Building Society in the year was £182.

If you require any further details please let me know.

Yours sincerely,

Adam Jones

Letters to Solicitors

237　Instructing a Solicitor to Prepare a Power of Attorney

110 Park Road,
Chalkerton,
Devon.
(postcode)
1st June 19--

Dear Mr Staples,

As I am going abroad next month and expect to be away for a year, I wish to give a general Power of Attorney to Mr Andrew Wells, 16 Homersham Villas, Brixham, to act for me, and on my behalf. Will you please draw up the necessary document and let me know when it is ready for signature.

Yours sincerely,
Jeremy Wheatley

238　Asking a Solicitor to Advance Money on a Legacy

110 Westgate Street,
Gloucester.
(postcode)
27th October 19--

Dear Sir,

With reference to your letter of 2nd August, informing me of the legacy left to me by my aunt, the late Miss Ethel Perkins, I should be glad to know when I am likely to receive this. I am in need of money at the moment and, if it will be some time before the matter is settled, I wonder if it would be possible for you to advance me £1000 of my legacy on account?

Yours faithfully,
Thomas Simkins

239   Asking a Solicitor to Advise about a Claim for Damages

101 FISHERMAN'S WHARF,
BRIXHAM,
DEVON.
(postcode)
15th August 19--

Dear Mr Donaldson,

I enclose a letter from a Mr Henry Root of London. You will see that he is claiming £2500 damages for injuries he received and the consequent loss of earnings he has sustained by a tile falling from my roof onto his head. Certainly the tile did fall on his head, and cut the scalp slightly. As far as I know, that is the only injury he suffered, but he he has been incapacitated for four months and claims for loss of wages during that period.

The tile was dislodged in a very strong gale and, as far as I can see, there is no evidence of negligence on my part. I sincerely hope that I am not liable for a claim of this sort, as I have no insurance policy that covers it.

Would you please let me know what reply I should make to this letter, and the best course of action for me to take.

Yours sincerely,

CHARLES WHITING

240   To a Solicitor, Giving Instructions for Alterations to a Will

101 THE GROVE,
EXETER.
(postcode)
12th September 19--

Dear Mr Curry,

I should like to make an alteration to the will which you drew up for me last year and which you hold. I wish to revoke the legacy to my godson, Max Hislop. If this can be done by a codicil, will you please draw up the document and send it to me for signature? The amount of the legacy is to go into the residue of the estate.

If this is not a matter for a simple codicil and you wish to see me, I must ask you to come here, as I regret that I am unable to come to your offices.

Yours sincerely,

ELIZABETH SANDERS

241 To a Friend, Asking him to Act as Executor

42 PALACE GARDENS,
BOGNOR REGIS,
SUSSEX.
(postcode)
30th June 19--

Dear Mark,

I am in the process of making a will, and would like to name you as joint Executor with Brenda. I know Brenda would like to have your help and advice if she needed it, and I know I could rely on you to carry out my wishes. It would not be an onerous task of course, for I have little to leave, but as you know my financial position I feel your help would be invaluable.

Yours ever,

KEITH

242 Instructing a Solicitor to Collect an Account

142 SWALLOW HILL,
ONGAR,
ESSEX.
(postcode)
18th June 19--

Dear Mr Brown,

Nine months ago I sold a motor-car to Mr Mark Stone of 15b Flint Rise, Warminster for an agreed price of £850. He paid £450 on the spot and undertook to pay the balance by eight monthly instalments of £50. I enclose his letter in which he agreed to this arrangement. I gave him possession of the car on payment of the £450, but have not received another penny from him. I have written to him repeatedly and he has ignored my letters. I now feel I have no alternative but to put the matter in your hands. Possibly a letter from you will bring him to his senses but, if not, please take whatever steps are necessary to recover the amount due to me. I am sure he is well able to pay.

Yours sincerely,

MICHAEL HILLS

Letters about Housing

243 To a Building Society, Applying for Shares with a View to Ultimate House Purchase

101 WAVELL COURT,
HENDON,
LONDON NW12.
15th May 19--

The Manager,

The ---- Building Society

Dear Sir,

I wish to start investing in your Society with a view ultimately to purchasing a house on mortgage. I would be grateful if you could send me all the relevant brochures, your rules and an application form for the shares most suited to my needs.

My investment would be, on average, £100 per month and my intended house purchase in about 3 years' time. At today's prices I shall be looking for a house in the £20–£25,000 price range. My current salary, as a Civil Servant, is £9000 p.a.

Yours faithfully,

RONALD SLIM

244   To a Building Society, Applying for a Mortgage

2 Cherry Lane,
Ingram,
Northumberland.
(postcode)
19th March 19--

The Manager
The ---- Building Society
Dear Sir,

Re: Share a/c No: ----------

I enclose an Estate Agent's prospectus of a property I am most anxious to purchase.

My shares in your Society, after three years' saving, have now reached £3600 and, as you will see, the purchase price of the house is £25,000. My present income, as a Civil Servant, is £8000 p.a.

I should be glad to know if you would be willing to advance the balance of £16,400 – this to be repaid by monthly instalments over the next 20 years.

The property can be surveyed at any time.

An early reply would be appreciated as there are several potential purchasers.

Yours faithfully,
S. K. Bridger

245   To a Building Society, Regarding House Purchase

174 Blossom Lane,
Nelson,
Lancashire.
(postcode)
4th January 19--

The Manager
The ---- Building Society
Dear Sir,

I am considering the purchase of a house in Hampshire at a price of £25,000 and wonder whether you would be prepared to advance 80% of the purchase price. The house is brick-built and slated, in an excellent condition and well situated, with an orchard and well-stocked garden.

You would, of course, require your surveyor to inspect it, and if you will let me have details of your terms, I should be pleased to accompany him there if I decide to carry the matter through.

I am a Builder and Decorator, with my own business, and have audited accounts for the past three years showing my average annual income to be £10,000. Apart from some small gilt-edged securities, I also have an Endowment Policy with the —————— Insurance Company for a sum assured of £5000 with profits. This policy has been running for the past 10 years and was originally taken out for a 20-year period.

Your early advice will be most welcome.

Yours faithfully,

Rex Warren

246   To a Building Society, Asking Terms to Pay off a Mortgage

149 Colin Court,

Narborough,

Norfolk.

(postcode)

16th May 19--

The Manager

The ———— Building Society

Dear Sir,

Account No. ——————

I am considering paying off the balance of my mortgage in a lump sum. Assuming your Society would agree to this, could you please let me know the exact amount outstanding. I am aware that most of my initial repayments were towards the Interest element on my loan and that I have only recently started paying off the remainder of the Capital element. Am I being wise to consider this lump sum repayment or should I re-invest my capital and continue paying off my mortgage on the present monthly basis?

Yours faithfully,

Thomas Bennett

247   To a Building Society, Withdrawing Money Invested

84 OPORTO AVENUE,
BURTON UPON TRENT.
(postcode)
9th October 19--

The Manager
The ---- Building Society
Dear Sir,

   I write to give seven days' notice, as required by Rule XXV, that I wish to withdraw the money paid on my shares in your Society. I enclose my book, which shows £690.93 to my credit, and I should be glad to have a cheque for this amount and any interest that is due to me.

Yours faithfully,

DAVID TEMPLE

248   Asking a Bank to Undertake a Search

45 PALMER ROAD,
NEW MALDEN,
SURREY.
(postcode)
26th May 19--

a/c No. . . . .

The Manager,
. . . . Bank
Dear Sir,

   I am having an extension built to my house at a cost of £20,000 and have received one or two estimates from builders. The one I have chosen is W. Brown & Sons of Kingston and I should be obliged if you would make an inquiry on their bankers as to the builder's general standing and suitability to carry out a contract for that amount in stage payments. I understand that the bank in question is . . . . Bank, Kingston.

Yours faithfully,

HUBERT JAMES

249   To a House Decorator, Asking for an Estimate

86 HORNSEY AVENUE,
HALE, LANCS.
(postcode)
28th February 19--

Messrs Farr & Fyfe Ltd

Dear Sirs,

I wish to have the outside of my house painted, back and front, and I should be obliged if you would send a representative to give an estimate of the cost. I should also like to know when you could carry out the work. Kindly ask your representative to telephone before calling, since I would like to discuss with him the most suitable type of paint for the job.

Yours faithfully,

M. JACKSON

250   To a Landlord, Asking for Repairs to be Done

15 ROSEMARY CLOSE,
KINGSTON,
SURREY.
(postcode)
12th November 19--

Dear Sir,

I believe that, under the terms of our lease, it is your responsibility to repair the front fence of this house. It is in a very dilapidated condition and is in danger of falling into the road, where it might injure someone.

I would appreciate it if you could send someone round to repair it.

Yours faithfully,

ELEANOR SAUNDERS

251   To a Landlord, Asking Permission to Sublet

159 BAINES ROAD,
KEIGHLEY.
(postcode)
21st February 19--

Dear Mr Leonard,

In these days of galloping inflation I am, like most others, finding it harder and harder to make ends meet. My situation would, of course, be much improved if I were to let the top floor of this house. Under the terms of our lease I see that I am able, with your permission, to sublet part of the house. I have found a most suitable tenant – a Mrs Alexander, a widow, and her daughter Emma, aged 29. They have excellent references from their former landlady, which I enclose. It would be a great relief to know that there is someone else in the house; I hope, therefore, that you will raise no objection and will be able to let me have your formal written consent as soon as possible.

Yours sincerely,

ANNE JENKINS(MRS)

252 To a Landlord, Asking for Time to Pay the Rent

114 KINSMAN STREET,
CHARLTON,
LONDON SE7.
21st January 19––

Dear Mr Bruce,

Owing to unexpected circumstances, of which you may have heard, I regret that at present I am unable to pay my rent for the next half-year. My embarrassment is only temporary and, as payment has always been punctually made, I hope you will see your way to letting it stand over for a month or two.

Yours sincerely,

JOHN WATSON

253 From a Landlord, Granting Time

10 MAUGHAM MANSIONS,
LONDON W1.
23rd January 19––

Dear Mr Watson,

As you assume, I have heard reports of your difficulties and I think you have known me long enough to be sure that I am not likely to be unreasonable to a tenant who has always made his payments punctually. When you can conveniently pay the next half-year's rent, do so, and you may be assured that I shall not press you for it for a few months. I hope that your difficulties will soon be satisfactorily overcome.

Yours sincerely,

DAVID BRUCE

254   From a Landlord, Refusing Time

10 MAUGHAM MANSIONS,
LONDON W1.
23rd January 19--

Dear Mr Watson,

I am sorry to hear of the difficult position in which you find yourself. If it were possible to grant you time to pay the rent now overdue, I would most willingly do so; but I have many and urgent calls upon me at this moment, and must therefore ask you to forward me the amount by return of post.

Yours sincerely,

DAVID BRUCE

255   To a House Agent, Asking him to Let a Furnished House

RIVERSIDE COTTAGE,
SANDWICH,
KENT.
(postcode)
1st March 19--

Dear Sir,

I should like to let this house furnished as a holiday letting for a period of 6 months from the end of this month at a rent of £---- a week. There are two reception rooms, four bedrooms, kitchen and bathroom, h & c water, and a good garden. It is well furnished, and I am willing to leave linen and cutlery if desired.

I should like to know if you think it possible to find me a suitable tenant and what your terms would be.

Yours faithfully,

PAULINE BLAND (MRS)

256   To A House Agent, Making an Offer for a Furnished Flat

15 Beechcroft Road,
Halesowen,
Worcs.
(postcode)
8th March 19--

Dear Sir,

I have seen over Flat 1, 10 Bouverie Gardens, Brighton, and should be glad to know if the owner would be willing to accept £---- per month if I guaranteed to take the flat for six months. In addition the enclosed list of articles which I consider necessary should be supplied.

Yours faithfully,

Penelope Ross (mrs)

257   To a House Agent, Inquiring for Flats

15 Nash Crescent,
Bath,
Avon.
(postcode)
12th May 19--

Dear Sir,

Would you please send me details of any unfurnished flats that you have on your books in the Barnes/Hammersmith area.

If you have none, I would be interested in receiving details of any two/three bedroom houses that you have for sale up to a price of £---.

Yours faithfully,

B. Abbott

Letters about Insurance

258   To an Insurance Company Regarding Motor-Car Insurance

CONSTANCE COTTAGE,
FENTON,
DEVON.
(postcode)
26th July 19--

The ---- Insurance Company Ltd,
London.

Dear Sirs,

I should like to buy a Ford Fiesta 1100 cc, but before doing so would be glad to have some idea of your motor policies. Could you let me know your terms for Comprehensive and Third Party Insurance, also the difference in cost between allowing the car to be driven by anyone with my consent, and restricting the drivers to my wife and myself?

I have been driving for five years without accident, but this will be the first car that I have owned. The car would be garaged at the above address and would be for private use only.

This information will be much appreciated.

Yours faithfully,

PETER SYKES

259   Reporting an Accident and Making a Claim under a Motoring Policy

147 CLOTH LANE,
WASHINGTON,
LANCS.
(postcode)
16th December 19--

Dear Sirs,

Re: Motor Policy No. -----

I would be grateful if you could send me a Claim Form as I was involved in an accident this morning.

The police have been informed and I have full details of the other driver – name, address, his insurance company etc. He has also admitted liability both to myself and to the police.

Yours faithfully,

PAMELA PRICE

260   Trying to Recover Costs after an Accident

NEWTON COTTAGE,

TROUTBECK,

CUMBRIA.

(postcode)

2nd January 19––

Dear Sir,

Following the accident which occurred between your car and mine at
. . . . . on . . . . . it is my understanding and your admission that the accident
was entirely your fault.

I now enclose a copy of an estimate of the cost of repair and a note of
the additional costs which I incurred solely as a result of the accident. As
my car is used, and insured, for business purposes it is necessary for me to
hire alternative transport while mine is under repair. I shall expect you
or your insurers to meet all these items of cost in full.

Would you please forward this letter to your insurers, who I believe to
be . . . . . .

I await word from them that they accept liability on your behalf.

Yours faithfully,

PAUL FISHER

261   To a Fire Insurance Company, Regarding Fire Insurance, etc., of a House

AMBROSE COTTAGE,

VERNEY,

GLOUCESTERSHIRE.

(postcode)

4th June 19––

Dear Sirs,

I wish to cover my house and effects against fire, etc. I believe you
have a policy which covers practically all risks, including Fire, Explosion,

168

Burst Water Pipes, Burglary, Accident to Third Parties. I should be glad to have details.

I should like to insure the building for £20,000 and the contents for £8000.

I further understand that it is possible to insure items that may be lost or stolen whilst 'outside the home'. Cameras, watches, rings etc. I gather the premium is greater for this type of cover but would be grateful for a guide to insuring £300, no one item to exceed £50 on an All Risks Policy.

Yours faithfully,

WILLIAM DUTTON

262   Making a Claim under a Burglary Policy

162 WALLACE ROAD,
BOXTED,
ESSEX.
(postcode)
19th November 19--

Claim: Burglary Policy No. . . . .

Dear Sirs,

This house was entered by burglars last night who took away a number of silver articles and jewellery. I have made out a list of articles which are missing, but there may be others. The list is enclosed and shows replacement values of the items.

As I am insured with you against loss by burglary and larceny, I write to claim the value of the articles stolen.

I have informed the police, who have inspected the premises and are pursuing inquiries.

Yours faithfully,

IAN DUNLOP

Letters to Tradesmen

263 To a Department Store, Asking to Open an Account

123 ROLLO STREET,
LONDON SW11.
14th February 19--

Sands & Rowland P.L.C.,
Clapham Junction, SW11.

Dear Sirs,

It would be a great convenience to me if I could open a credit account with your firm. Please could you let me know how this may be arranged. I bank at the National Westminster Bank, Park Road and Mrs Fremantle of 101 Macdonald Way or Mrs Parry, of 71b Clapham Gardens would be prepared to vouch for me if personal references are required. I look forward to hearing from you.

Yours faithfully,
BEATRICE YOUNG

264 Refusing Unsolicited Goods

1234 WESTOVER ROAD,
NANTON,
CHESHIRE.
(postcode)
21st February 19--

The Slikway Recording Co.,
Milburn,
Lancs.

Dear Sirs,

I received from you today two cassettes which I did not order and I do not want. If you care to send me 95p to cover the cost of the postage, I will return them to you. Failing that, I shall give them to a jumble sale. Please ensure that I do not receive any more unsolicited goods from your firm.

Yours faithfully,
CONSTANCE FENTON (MRS)

265   Complaining of Delay in Delivery of Goods

410 Radnor Walk,
Lismore,
Cornwall.
(postcode)
1st June 19--

Clegg & Co. Ltd,
Florists,
Bude.

Dear Sirs,

On 16th May I ordered from you a number of indoor plants and was promised delivery within a week. Two weeks have now passed but the plants have not arrived despite the fact that I have telephoned twice and on each occasion have been told that the matter would be dealt with at once. The plants are required as decoration for a party I am giving on 6th June. If you are unable to dispatch them on immediate receipt of this letter, please cancel the order and I will take my business elsewhere.

Yours faithfully,

Patricia Simmonds (mrs)

266   To a Laundry, Complaining of Loss

124 Crooked Lane,
Shawcross,
Bucks.
(postcode)
29th July 19--

The Manager,
The Marina Laundry Ltd,
Staines.

Dear Sir,

I rang you on Tuesday to point out that two of my husband's new shirts were missing from last week's laundry. As they are not in this week's parcel I assume that you have been unable to trace them, so I must ask you to refund their value, which is £12.95 each. I have no doubt that I can obtain a duplicate invoice from the shop where they were bought if required.

Yours faithfully,

Doreen Hume (mrs)

267 To a Garage, Asking for an Estimate

151 CLEESE LANE,
LONDON SW12.
18th JANUARY 19--

G. Phillips Ltd,
148 Culvert Road,
London SW11.

Dear Sirs,

My car licence expires next month and I need an MOT certificate before I can get it relicensed. If I bring the car in on Monday week (28th), could you let me have an estimate for servicing and for carrying out the MOT test? I do not think there is anything radically wrong with the vehicle.

Yours faithfully,
NIGEL HART

Letters about Education

268 To the Secretary of a School, Asking for Particulars

83 SUTTON STREET,
LONDON SW6.
12th October 19--

The Secretary,
Hastings House School.

Dear Madam,

I should be most grateful if you would send me a prospectus of Hastings House. My daughter, Melanie, will be 11 next May (19--) and would therefore be ready for entry in the following September.

Melanie suffers slightly from asthma and as we live in London we feel she would benefit from the sea air at Hastings.

Yours faithfully,
JANE PIGGOTT

269 To the Secretary of a School, Arranging an Appointment

83 SUTTON STREET,
LONDON SW6.
17th October 19--

The Secretary,
Hastings House School.

Dear Miss Stevenson,

Thank you for your letter of the 15th enclosing a prospectus.

You suggested 14th November at 11 a.m. as a possible time at which we could meet the headmistress and see round the school. As we come from London this is a little early for us, and I wonder if we could make it 11.30 a.m. Unless I hear to the contrary, I shall assume that this is convenient to you.

We much look forward to meeting Miss Drury.

Yours sincerely,

JANE PIGGOTT

270 To the Principal of a School Entering a Daughter

83 SUTTON STREET,
LONDON SW6.
15th November 19--

The Headmistress,
Hastings House School.

Dear Miss Drury,

Thank you very much for giving up your time to talk to us yesterday. My husband and I were both impressed with your school and feel sure that Melanie would be happy with you.

I therefore return the completed entrance form, together with £10 registration fee. We will bring Melanie down for the entrance examination on 30th January as arranged.

Yours sincerely,

JANE PIGGOTT

271 Accepting a Place at a School

83 SUTTON STREET,
LONDON SW6.
20th March 19--

The Headmistress,
Hastings House School.

Dear Miss Drury,

We were delighted to hear that Melanie had done so well in her entrance examination and are pleased to accept your offer of a place in September. I enclose £50 deposit as requested.

Yours sincerely,

JANE PIGGOTT

272 Withdrawing a Child from a School

83 SUTTON STREET,
LONDON SW6.
12th July 19--

The Headmistress,
Hastings House School.

Dear Miss Drury,

After a year of struggling to help Melanie settle down with you, I am afraid we must concede defeat. I had hoped that, after the initial home-sickness of the first term, Melanie might learn to enjoy all that your school has to offer. Unfortunately she is obviously miserable and as her asthma seems to get progressively worse, I think it would be better if we brought her home and sent her to a day school.

I am deeply grateful for all your concern and care for Melanie and I do hope you won't feel that this reflects badly on you in any way. I think Melanie's physical problems make her over-sensitive and less able to cope outside her home environment.

Yours sincerely,

JANE PIGGOTT

273 To a Headmaster, Requesting Extra Tuition

18 PARK AVENUE,
CHICHESTER,
W. SUSSEX.
(postcode)
30th March 19--

The Headmaster,
Sussex Comprehensive School.

Dear Mr Hunt,

I wonder whether it would be possible for James to start learning Spanish next term. I realize that the boys do not usually start a second language until the fourth year, but as my husband is shortly being posted to Argentina, it would obviously be useful for James to have some knowledge of Spanish. I am prepared to pay for out-of-school lessons should this prove necessary.

Yours sincerely,

PAULINE GRAHAM

274 To a Headmaster, Complaining of Bullying

47 KERSLEY STREET,
MARTLEY,
WORCS.
(postcode)
5th October 19--

The Headmaster,
Bolingbroke Park School.

Dear Mr Seymour,

Twice this week my son Gary has come home, bruised and distressed, having been attacked by boys from your school on the way home. Being new to the school he does not know their names and is terrified of retribution should he complain to you.

I realize that, outside the school, the boys are out of your jurisdiction, but I wonder whether it would be possible for you to take some action. Should this be impossible, and should the attacks continue, I shall have no alternative but to report the matter to the police.

Yours sincerely,

MAVIS NEWLAND

275 Thanking a Headmaster

47 KERSLEY STREET,
MARTLEY,
WORCS.
(postcode)
20th August 19--

Dear Mr Seymour,

I should like to thank you for making my seven years at Bolingbroke Park so happy. Without your inspiration and, dare I say it, bullying to make me work, I should never have done so well in my A Levels, nor

175

I have achieved a place at Leeds. I can't thank you enough, and 〔ho〕pe I shall do you justice when I continue my studies at university.

Yours sincerely,

GARY NEWLAND

276 To the British Council, Asking for Information about Scholarships

193 ISABEL LA CATOLICA,
SANTIAGO,
CHILE.
5th June 19--

The Education Department,
The British Council,
Santiago.

Dear Sir,

I am at present a research student at the Catholic University here, studying the causes of liver disease in children. I am anxious to have the opportunity of further study in London, where I believe King's College Hospital is doing pioneering work in the treatment of infantile liver disorders. I understand that the British Council gives scholarships for foreign students to study in English universities and hospitals. Would you be kind enough to let me have some information about this so that I can find out if I am eligible to apply?

Yours faithfully,

EMILIO LOPES

277 To the Chief Education Officer of a County, Applying for a Grant

69 BATH ROAD,
TROWBRIDGE,
WILTSHIRE.
5th August 19--

The Education Officer,
Education Department,
The Town Hall,
Trowbridge,
Wiltshire.

Dear Sir,

I have just been offered a place at Bristol University to study for a BA in history and believe I might qualify for a grant as a mature student. I

176

left Chippenham Girl's School four years ago and have been working as an Assistant Librarian at Bath Library since then. I have A Levels in History, English and Latin (Grades A, A+ B, respectively), and have lived in Trowbridge for the last 10 years. If I am likely to qualify for a grant, would you kindly send me any necessary information, including application forms.

Yours faithfully,

KATHERINE BATES

278   To the British Council, Asking for Information about Books

Egypt.

7th June 19--

The Librarian,
The British Council,
Cairo.

Dear Sir,

I am teaching English to a group of young men from this village. We are rather short of simple reading material and wonder whether you could suggest suitable books or magazines for us. Easily written novels or detective stories are always popular, and we should like to have some books which would give us an idea of life in England.

Your help would be very much appreciated.

Yours faithfully,

M. ALI

279   From a Foreign Student, Asking about Applying for Entrance to an English University

Nigeria.

1st May 19--

The Education Officer,
The British Council,
Lagos.

Dear Sir,

I am anxious to enter an English university to study Computer Technology. I wonder if you could let me know which universities have suitable courses, how I apply and what qualifications I should need for entry.

Yours faithfully,

BOLA OGOJA

References and Introductions

280 From a School Leaver, Applying for a Reference

197 WESTON ROAD,
OLDFIELD,
LANCS.
(postcode)
21st July 19--

Geoffrey Neville Esq.,
Neville Service Station Ltd.

Dear Mr Neville,

I have just applied for a job as a trainee mechanic at Moberley Watt Garage, which is at 15 York Road. This would be my first full-time job and Mr Watt is anxious to have evidence of my work experience. As I worked for you during the last summer holidays, I wonder if you would kindly write a reference for me. I much enjoyed working for you and I do hope you can fulfil my request.

Yours sincerely,

GARY NEWLANDS

281 From a Companion, Applying for a Reference

51 BATH ROAD,
YEOVIL,
SOMERSET.
(postcode)
9th April 19--

Dear Mrs Hunt,

I have recently applied for a job as companion to Mrs Armitage of The Grange, Compton. As you knew me well when I was working for

Mrs Skinner, I wonder if I might quote you as a reference. My duties with Mrs Armitage would be very similar to those I fulfilled for Mrs Skinner and I think I can say, with due modesty, that Mrs Skinner was happy in my company.

I haven't worked since Mrs Skinner's sad death last year so I would be particularly grateful if you could help me in this way.

Yours sincerely,

JANET CHIVERS

282   Asking for an Introduction

15 WESTON PLACE,
LONDON SW1.
3rd June 19--

Dear M. André,

I do hope that you will not mind me writing to ask for your help. My firm are shortly transferring me to our French office and at the end of this week my wife and I are off to live in Paris – probably for the next two years. I shall be fully occupied with my work but I am rather concerned about my wife. Her French is very limited, although she is already trying to brush it up, and I fear that initially she may find life both difficult and lonely. I wonder if, knowing as you do so many people in Paris, you could give her introductions to any young wives of about her age, preferably speaking some English. Forgive me for troubling you, but I would be most grateful for any help which you can give us. Incidentally my office number in Paris will be -------.

Yours sincerely,

ROGER RUSHTON

283   Introducing a Stranger to a Friend

6 MOSSOP SQUARE,
LONDON SW1.
10th June 19--

Dear Claudette,

Two young friends of mine, Roger and Annabel Rushton, have just moved to Paris where he has been sent by his firm. I wonder if you would kindly ask them round and, if you like them, which I'm sure you will, introduce them to a few people. She is very pretty but rather shy. He is extremely intelligent and most amusing. Roger can be contacted at his office, the telephone number of which is −−−−−.

Yours ever,

GÉRARD

284 Introducing a Stranger to an Acquaintance

6 MOSSOP SQUARE,
LONDON SW1.
10th June 19−−

Dear M. Martin,

I hope you will forgive me for troubling you but I wonder if you could do me a great favour. Two young friends of mine have just arrived in Paris where they will be living for the next two years. As they will be strangers in a strange city any kindness you can show them will be much appreciated by them, and by me. Their names are Roger and Annabel Rushton. Roger can be contacted at his office, the telephone number of which is −−−−−−.

Yours sincerely,

GÉRARD ANDRÉ

285 To an English Acquaintance in a Foreign Country, Asking her to Visit her Young Daughter who is Staying There

APRIL COTTAGE,
RYE, SUSSEX.
(postcode)
10th August 19−−

Dear Francesca,

You will be surprised to hear from me after such a long time and it embarrasses me to have to confess that it is because I need your help that I am at last inspired to write to you.

My 18-year-old daughter, Maxine, who must have been about 12 when you last saw her, is staying with a family in Florence in order to learn Italian. She has been there for a fortnight and it appears from her letters that she is very unhappy. It was originally intended that she

180

should stay for six months, but this is out of the question if she is really miserable. I don't know the family she is staying with but I made careful inquiries and everything seemed suitable and satisfactory. I expect that much of the trouble is homesickness and I don't want to panic and let her come home unnecessarily.

I know that you go into Florence two or three times a week and I wonder if you would be very kind and take her out for a cup of coffee one morning and find out what is wrong. I would be extremely grateful and it would take a great weight off my mind. Her address is c/o Guidotti, 1280 Via Cerretani.

I hope that you and Gianfranco are keeping well.

Yours ever,

MARIETTA

286 Requesting a Friend to Call on an Acquaintance

BAGLEY COTTAGE,
STOKENHAM,
DEVON.
(postcode)
10th September 19--

My dear Brenda,

Some friends of ours have just bought a house quite close to you and I'd be most grateful if you could ask them over for a cup of coffee or a drink some time, as they don't know many people in your area. They are Jack and Jemma Gutteridge and their new address is Banks Cottage, Bradford-on-Avon. I have no telephone number yet. Jack works for Herbert's company and has been moved to the Bath office. They are both extremely nice and I'm sure that you will like them very much.

Love from

MARGARET

287 To a Doctor, Saying Goodbye and Asking for an Introduction

81 ERROLL DRIVE,
NAIROBI.
8th September 19--

Dear Dr Oneko,

As you know, my husband and I are leaving Nairobi soon and moving to Malindi. I cannot go away without writing to tell you how grateful we both are for your kindness to us since we have been your patients.

May I ask you one last favour? Could you possibly recommend us to a good doctor in Malindi and, if it is not too much trouble, perhaps give us a letter of introduction?

With many thanks,

Yours sincerely,

ALICE MWENDA

288   Asking for a Reference

5 PENNY LANE,
HARBURY,
WARWICKSHIRE.
(postcode)
25th February 19--

Dear Mr Dixon,

Mr William Tute has applied to me for a job as a part-time gardener and has given your name as a reference. He tells me that he was employed by you in a similar capacity for five years from 1965 to 1970.

I should be much obliged if you could tell me whether you found him a satisfactory and trustworthy worker and why he left your employment. Naturally I shall treat anything you tell me in the strictest confidence. I enclose a stamped and addressed envelope.

Yours sincerely,

EDWARD VOLES

289   Giving a Favourable Reference

Private and Confidential

TROOPER'S REST,
SHIPSTON-ON-STOUR.
(postcode)
28th February 19--

Dear Mr Voles,

In answer to your letter about William Tute, I can give you my unqualified assurance that you would be hard put to it to find a better worker, a more trustworthy or more willing and friendly man. He left here when his wife died to go and live with his sister. We were very sorry to say goodbye to him. Please give him my kind regards.

Yours sincerely,
MATTHEW DIXON

290   Giving a Qualified Reference

Private and Confidential

TROOPER'S REST,
SHIPSTON-ON-STOUR.
(postcode)
28th February 19--

Dear Mr Voles,

In answer to your letter about William Tute, I can assure you that he is both hard-working and trustworthy. He does, however, need to be told exactly what to do and, as I am away for much of the year, I found it impossible to give him the supervision necessary. If you are on hand to show him what to do, you will find him an excellent worker.

Yours sincerely,
MATTHEW DIXON

291   Another Qualified Reference

Private and Confidential

TROOPER'S REST,
SHIPSTON-ON-STOUR.
(postcode)
28th February 19--

Dear Mr Voles,

Mr Tute worked for me as a part-time gardener for five years and I have no hesitation in saying that he is a hard-working and altogether trustworthy man. Unfortunately his health failed and after he had been in hospital for six months I was obliged to engage someone else. Provided that he is now fully recovered, I'm sure you will find him quite satisfactory.

Yours sincerely,
MATTHEW DIXON

292 Refusing a Reference

Private and Confidential

TROOPER'S REST,
SHIPSTON-ON-STOUR.
(postcode)
28th February 19--

Dear Mr Voles,

I write to confirm that Mr Tute did indeed work for me for five years. I'm afraid, however, that I would rather say no more and must leave you to draw your own conclusions.

Yours sincerely,
MATTHEW DIXON

293 From a Previous Employer Asking not to be Referred to

Private and Confidential

TROOPER'S REST,
SHIPSTON-ON-STOUR.
(postcode)
28th February 19--

Dear Tute,

I have received a letter from a Mr Voles, asking me to give you a reference. Bearing in mind the circumstances under which you left my employment, I cannot understand how you could have imagined that it would be to your advantage to give my name. I would be grateful if you would not do so again.

Yours,
MATTHEW DIXON

294 To a Friend Asking him to Act as Referee

DINGLEY DELL COTTAGE,
SHERBORNE.
(postcode)
27th July 19--

Dear Charles,

I have applied for a job as Caretaker in a large house in Scotland, the owners of which live abroad during most of the year. The duties consist

184

of keeping an eye on the place in their absence and seeing that all is in order whenever they return. They have asked for two references and I wondered if I might give your name as one. I hope you will feel able to say that Lucy and I are reasonably honest and sober citizens!

Yours ever,

ANDY

295   From a Gentleman Giving a Reference

CEDAR LODGE,
ALDSWORTH.
(postcode)
1st August 19--

Dear Mr Freeman,

I have known Mr and Mrs Verney for the past 35 years and I can assure you that you would be hard pressed to find a more honest, reliable and intelligent couple to look after your property in your absence.

Yours sincerely,

CHARLES BURFORD

Letters about Travel and Holidays

296   To a Travel Agent Asking for Details of a Package Tour

172 PALMERSTON STREET,
MARTON,
CHESHIRE.
(postcode)
14th March 19--

Globewise Travel Ltd,
178 Fulham Road,
London SW6.

Dear Sirs,

I have seen your advertisement offering two weeks holiday in Tunisia for an all-in cost of £235 per head. Please could you let me have the following additional details: (1) Is it possible at the same time to visit Algeria and Libya? If so, will additional documentation be required? (2) Is it better to change one's money in this country or to take travellers' cheques? (3) Are any inoculations or injections required for Tunisia, Libya or Algeria? (4) What is the temperature likely to be at this time of year?

Yours faithfully,

JUNE BARFORD (MRS)

297 To a Travel Agency Asking them to Arrange Local Tours

2271 PULLAVARAM DRIVE,
MADRAS,
INDIA.
15th January 19--

John Peters Ltd,
Shepherd Market,
London W1.

Dear Sirs,

My wife and I will be arriving in London on 13 March next and will be staying for three weeks. We should like to book seats on coach tours enabling us to visit Althorp, Windsor, Stratford, Longleat and Salisbury. Could you let us have the necessary timetables so that we can make our plans and ask you to book the seats required.

Yours faithfully

B.K. CHOPRA

298 To a Travel Agent Asking him to Book Car Space on a Ferry

121 DOYLE AVENUE,
BRISTOL.
(postcode)
12th April 19--

John Peters Ltd,
Shepherd Market,
London W1.

Dear Sirs,

I should be grateful if you could book space for my car on any ferry crossing from Dover to Calais on the afternoon of 14 May between 1400 and 16.30 hrs. The car is a Ford Fiesta 1100, registration no. DPD 732 T. Please let me know the time of sailing and how long in advance one has to report. I intend to travel through Belgium and West Germany to München and then on to Vienna. Can you also let me know what documentation I require.

Yours faithfully,
JOHN PERRY

299   To a Landlady Asking about Holiday Flats

175 GILLON ROAD,
BRYNMAWR,
POWYS.
(postcode)
15th March 19--

Dear Madam,

Would you be kind enough to let me know whether you still have any rooms available in the month of August? We should be a party of four – my husband, myself, my son Daniel, aged 14, and my daughter Rachel, aged 10. We should need a double bedroom, two single bedrooms and a sitting-room, with service. We should like, if possible, to stay for three weeks from 30th July.

I was given your name and address by my neighbour, Mrs Reed, who, as you will doubtless remember, stayed with you for two weeks last summer. She thoroughly enjoyed her holiday.

I enclose a stamped and addressed envelope for your reply and, if you are not already fully booked, would be grateful if you could let me know your terms.

Yours faithfully,
PRISCILLA BUTT (MRS)

300   To a Town Clerk Asking for Information about a Seaside Town

> 176 HOLDSWORTH ROAD,
> MANNING,
> CHESHIRE.
> (postcode)
> *12th January 19--*

The Town Clerk,
Rockerby-on-Sea.

Dear Sir,

   Would you kindly supply me with, or let me know how I can obtain, a list of furnished accommodation to rent in Rockerby during the holiday season. I should also be grateful if you could send any guides, brochures or other leaflets which are available.

> With many thanks,
> Yours faithfully,
> JANE SIMMONDS

301   Booking Rooms

> 64 DYKE'S CROSS ROAD,
> CLIFFSIDE,
> BRISTOL.
> (postcode)
> *11th April 19--*

Dear Mrs Parry,

   Thank you for your letter of the 17th March provisionally reserving me one double bedroom for the fortnight starting 27th August. I note that your price is £74 per week inclusive of breakfast and evening meal. I enclose a deposit of £50 and would ask you to acknowledge receipt thereof. We shall be arriving at approximately 6.30 p.m. on the 27th.

> Yours sincerely,
> YVONNE WILLIAMS (MRS)

Letters to and from Club Secretaries

302   Applying for Membership of a Club

22 ACACIA LANE,
MERSTHAM, SURREY.
(postcode)
4th June 19--

The Hon. Secretary,
Ruskin Lawn Tennis Club.

Dear Sir,

My wife and I have recently come to live in the neighbourhood and would very much like to join the Ruskin Lawn Tennis Club. Unfortunately we do not know any of the members and wonder if you would be prepared to dispense with the introductions which most clubs require. We are both experienced players and for several years were members of the Achilles Club at Hove.

Yours faithfully,

LESLIE TURNER

303   Reply, Accepting Application

RUSKIN LAWN TENNIS CLUB,
MERSTHAM.
(postcode)
6th June 19--

Dear Mr Turner,

In reply to your letter of 4th June, it is, as you surmised, the normal practice of this Club for candidates to be proposed for election by at least two members. However, since you and your wife have been members of such a distinguished Club as the Achilles, it is my intention to ask the Committee at our next meeting, being held on 10th July, if they will consider making an exception in your case.

Perhaps you would both like to come to the club one evening before that date and have a drink with me and meet one or two of the members.

Yours sincerely,

JAMES HATCH (MAJOR)

304   To the Secretary, Proposing a Friend as Member

69 Raven Court,
McCall Street,
London SE22.
1st October 19--

Dear Mr Peel,

I would like to propose my friend Dermot Briggs of 22 Pollock St, Dulwich, for membership of the Chester Row Bridge Club. Mr Hugh Bredon has agreed to second him. Would you be kind enough to put his name up for election at the next committee meeting? I have known Mr Briggs for a number of years; he is a keen and accomplished player and will, I am sure, be a popular member of the club.

Yours sincerely,

Anthony Herbert

305   To the Secretary, Making a Complaint

212 Slapton Lane,
Kingsbridge,
Devon.
(postcode)
5th August 19--

Dear Sir,

May I draw your attention to the manner in which Rule 22 is blatantly disregarded by many members of the Yacht Club. The rule, as I need not tell you, categorically states that members may *not* bring children under 12 into the upstairs bar and lounge. Nowadays, however, it is impossible to have a drink there without being disturbed by small children racing in and out between the tables, the situation being particularly bad at week-ends. While in no way wishing to discourage members with young families from using the club, I see no reason why they should not be obliged to observe the rules and confine their children to those parts of the club specifically set aside for them.

I would be most grateful if you would raise the matter with the Committee at their next meeting.

Yours faithfully,

Alastair Garrett

Miscellaneous Letters

306 To a Friend Asking for a Loan

8 MAYFAIR MEWS,
LONDON WC1.
5th June 19--

Dear Mustapha,

As you know, my house was burgled the other day and, among other things, I lost £350 which I had put in a drawer and was intending to use for paying some overdue bills. Could you possibly lend me £350 until the end of next month? I should be able to repay you by then. I am asking you by letter because it is less awkward for you to refuse that way.

Yours ever,

HUSSAIN

307 Reply, Granting Loan

19 JOHN'S AVENUE,
GOLDERS GREEN,
LONDON N8.
6th June 19--

Dear Hussain,

I am delighted to have the opportunity to help as good a friend as yourself. Here is a cheque for £350. Pay me back when it is convenient.

Yours ever,

MUSTAPHA

308 Reply, Refusing Loan

19 JOHN'S AVENUE,
GOLDERS GREEN,
LONDON N8.
7th June 19--

Dear Hussain,

I would gladly have lent you £350 if I had it, but unfortunately I am very short myself at the moment. So sorry.

Yours ever,

MUSTAPHA

309 Request for Repayment of Loan

19 JOHN'S AVENUE,
GOLDERS GREEN,
LONDON N8.
1st September 19--

Dear Hussain,

I don't like to worry you but it is now 6 months since you borrowed £350 from me and I would hate the matter to cloud our friendship. Could you do something about it?

Yours ever,

MUSTAPHA

310 To a Friend in Financial Straits, Enclosing a Cheque

THE MILL HOUSE,
GORHAMBURY,
ST ALBANS.
(postcode)
1st March 19--

My dear Margaret,

I want you to do me a favour and allow me to send you a little help. In these inflationary times one does not need to be blessed with second sight to realize what an appalling strain upon your finances your mother's illness must be. Robert and I, as I'm sure you are aware, have more than enough money to satisfy our needs, so I hope that you will be sensible and accept the enclosed cheque without argument. If you prefer, you can regard it as a loan, but one which there is absolutely no need to repay until you can do so without the slightest inconvenience to yourself. I know how wonderfully you have looked after your mother and you will be giving me very great pleasure by allowing me to help you.

With much love,

NORMA

311   From a Widow to a Friend of her Late Husband Requesting a Loan

17 GLADSTONE ROAD,
TONBRIDGE,
KENT.
(postcode)
18th December 19--

Dear Stephen,

I find myself in rather an awkward situation and am writing to you, as you were without doubt George's closest friend, to ask if you can help me. As you know, George looked after all our financial affairs and already, in the short time since his death, I seem to have got into a muddle. Could you possibly lend me £500 for two or three months? I can repay you as soon as probate is granted, but I don't want to ask the solicitors, as they make everything so unnecessarily long-winded and complicated. I do hope that you won't mind me asking for your help.

Much love,

ALICE

312   From a Lady Asking for a Subscription

12 VICARAGE CRESCENT,
GODALMING,
SURREY.
(postcode)
14th November 19--

Dear Mrs Lee,

I know so well that sinking feeling you will already be experiencing on reading these first few words and realizing that you have just opened yet another begging letter, but I hope that you will, nevertheless, bear with me and read a little bit further.

As I expect you know, the Barton House Nursing Home is largely supported by the income from past legacies and by the fund-raising efforts of the committee. During the past few years, however, costs have risen so sharply that unless something is done very soon the Home may well have to close and the residents be rehoused in other establishments – which, I'm sure you will agree, would be a tragedy. So I am writing to you on behalf of the committee to ask if you would be kind enough to make a subscription, however small, to help keep the home going. Should you feel like making a covenant, I should be happy to send you the necessary form.

Yours sincerely,

SYLVIA DAVIS

313   Asking a Lady of Title to Open a Fête

THE CLOSE,
PRESTEIGNE,
POWYS,
WALES.
1st April 19--

Dear Lady Grandison,

I am writing to ask if you would be willing to open the Church Fête, which is being held in the Rectory garden on 18th July. There is no need to make a long speech, but a few words about the church roof and the urgent need for its repair, to which the funds raised will be devoted, might be apposite.

Your generous support, and that of Sir Henry, has meant a great deal to us in the past, and I hope that I can count on you once again.

Yours sincerely,

JENKYN EVANS,
Rector

314   Asking an Actress to Open a Fête

THE RECTORY,
PARLEIGH,
HAMPSHIRE.
(postcode)
1st April 19--

Dear Miss de Brett,

I don't need to tell you how proud all of us here in Parleigh are of your well-earned success and hope that I can prevail upon you to open our Church Fête, to be held in the Rectory garden on 18th July. There is no need to make a speech but if you could just say a few words and mention the church roof, to the repair of which the funds raised are being devoted, we can be confident that the fête will get off to a flying start.

I should add that I am writing to you with the unanimous agreement of the committee who fervently hope that you will be willing to open this fête.

Yours sincerely,
ROGER HOLLOWAY
Rector

315   Asking a Lady to Help at a Sale

20 RICHMOND ROAD,
KINGSTON.
(postcode)
24th September 19--

Dear Mrs Murray,

I have been asked to assist in organizing a sale of books and toys in aid of the fund for the restoration of St Mary's, and write to you in the hope of enlisting your aid. I feel sure that your interest will be aroused by the object, and I know how valuable your help and advice would be. We are having a meeting here at 4.00 p.m. next Monday. I do hope you will be able to come.

Yours sincerely,
ELEANOR SAUNDERS

316   To a Neighbour who is soon to Leave the District, Sending a Farewell Present

1 COMMON ROAD,
LONDON SW11.
4th October 19--

Dear Frances,

I'm sure that I don't need to tell you how much you and Nick will be missed in Battersea and how very sad Michael and I are that you are leaving. I do hope that you will come and visit us as often as you can and that the enclosed will help to remind you of the happy times we have had together.

With much love,
SUSIE

317 Acknowledgement

20B BRIDGE ROAD,
LONDON SW11.
8th October 19--

My dear Susie,

I can't tell you how touched Nick and I were by your sweet letter and lovely present. We send you both our warmest thanks.

We are very sad to be leaving but Nick has to go where his job dictates. We shall miss you very much but I promise that we shall keep in touch.

With much love,

FRANCES

318 To a Friend on Passing an Examination

57 SOUTH ROAD,
BARHAM,
KENT.
(postcode)
2nd August 19--

My dear Ingrid,

I have just heard from Ben the excellent news of your exam results and cannot resist writing to congratulate you. I must admit that I am not in the least surprised, but I am delighted for you. You must be feeling very proud of yourself – and with every reason. Well done, indeed!

Much love,

WENDY

319 Acknowledgement

VALE COTTAGE,
CORBETT,
KENT.
(postcode)
7th August 19--

Dear Wendy,

Many thanks for your kind letter. It is very good of you to say that you were not surprised. I certainly was! I can only imagine that whoever corrected my papers must have just won the pools or have been offered a post in California! I don't have to tell you how relieved I am that it is all over!

Much love,

INGRID

320   To an Acquaintance Who has been Knighted

17 PRIMROSE MANSIONS,
CHELTENHAM,
GLOUCESTERSHIRE.
(postcode)
28th June 19--

Dear Sir Douglas,

I have just heard of the honour that has been bestowed upon you and send you my very warmest congratulations. It is an honour which you richly deserve and I can think of no one more fitted to bear it and to do it credit. I know that you have not sought it, and possibly did not desire it, but I hope that it will give you pleasure.

Please give my kindest regards to Lady Sutherland; she must be very proud of you.

Yours sincerely,

ROBIN JARMAN

321   To a Vicar, Asking for News of a Parishioner

51 QUEENSGATE,
EASTBOURNE,
SUSSEX.
(postcode)
15th April 19--

The Rev. Canon Donald Crawford, MA,
The Vicarage,
North Melling,
Kent.

Dear Canon Crawford,

I must begin by offering you my sincere apologies for writing to you as a perfect stranger and asking for your assistance, but I know of no one

197

who could give me the information I require except, possibly, yourself.

I am anxious to get in touch with a man named Arthur Banks who, some years ago, was employed by a firm of which I am a director. One of the few things that I can remember about him is that he, or his family, once lived in North Melling. If you or any of your parishioners remember him or his family, and could put me in touch with him, I should be extremely obliged to you. I may add that my reason for wishing to contact Mr Banks is much to his advantage. I enclose a stamped envelope.

Yours sincerely,

OLIVER KINGSTON

322 To a Health Inspector, Complaining of a Public Nuisance

101 HAMPTON ROAD,
LONDON SW11.
1st July 19--

To the Health Inspector,
Wandsworth Borough Council,
Wandsworth Town Hall.

Dear Sir,

I write to draw your attention to the ever-growing mountain of rubbish on the vacant plot in Ivy Street. Unless the rubbish is cleared very soon and the area properly sealed off, the situation will deteriorate until what is now merely smelly and unsightly, becomes a major health hazard. As a ratepayer, I urge you to act promptly in the interest of all those living in the vicinity.

Yours faithfully,

WILLIAM HALLETT

323 Complaining to a Neighbour of a Nuisance

274 PENFOLD RISE,
GIPSY HILL,
LONDON SE12.
25th June 19--

Dear Larry,

I find the subject of this letter rather embarrassing, which is why I thought it better to write to you in the first instance, rather than raise the matter to your face.

The fact is that my wife and I are finding the noise from your children's record player increasingly hard to bear. It seems as if the noise gets louder and louder, and goes on later and later; and the sound comes through the party wall as if it were made of paper.

I think you will agree that in the past we have proved good neighbours to each other and I would hate there to be any ill-feeling or misunderstanding between us; but if you could have a word with your children and ask them if they could possibly turn the volume down a bit, you would be doing us a great favour.

Yours,

ROGER

324   Neighbour's Friendly Reply

272 PENFOLD RISE,
GIPSY HILL,
LONDON SE12.
26th June 19--

Dear Roger,

How restrained of you to write such a tactful letter! I'm terribly sorry that the kids' record player has been disturbing you. It certainly disturbs me and I am constantly telling them to turn the confounded thing down. I expect that the trouble is mostly when I am out in the evenings. I shall do my very best to see that you are not troubled in the future.

Yours ever,

LARRY

325   Complaining to a Neighbour of a Nuisance

75 BLENHEIM GARDENS,
SUTTON COLDFIELD.
25th June 19--

Dear Mr McCarthy,

I wonder if you could possibly ask your children to be a little more careful when roller-skating along the pavement. On several occasions in the past few weeks they have almost knocked down either my wife or myself; and I have witnessed near collisions with a number of other people. It cannot be long before there is a serious accident.

Yours sincerely,
DENNIS NAPIER

326 Neighbour's Unfriendly Reply

60 BLENHEIM GARDENS,
SUTTON COLDFIELD.
29th June 19--

Dear Mr Napier,

As dozens of children roller-skate on the pavement round here, no good will be served by me preventing my children from doing so. In any case the pavement is as much theirs as it is yours. If you feel so strongly about it, I suggest you get in touch with the police.

Yours sincerely,
NOËL MCCARTHY

APPENDICES

Forms of Address

for beginning, ending and addressing
official and social letters

The editors acknowledge their indebtedness to Patrick Montague-Smith's invaluable book *Debrett's Correct Form* in the compilation of this section, which, nevertheless, contains only the barest outlines. Those in need of more detailed information are advised to consult Mr Montague-Smith's book, the authoritative work on the subject.

1 Royalty

The Queen

Beginning of Letter Officially
Madam,
With my humble duty,
Ending
I have the honour to remain, Madam,
Your Majesty's most humble and obedient subject,
Envelope
Her Majesty the Queen, *or*
The Queen's Most Excellent Majesty (for formal or State documents).

The Queen Mother

In all respects as in the case of the Queen.
Envelope
Her Gracious Majesty Queen Elizabeth, the Queen Mother.

Other Members of the Royal Family

Beginning
Sir *or* Madam
Ending
I have the honour to be, Sir (*or* Madam),
Your Royal Highness's most humble and obedient servant,
Envelope
His Royal Highness the Duke of . . . ., *or*
Her Royal Highness the Duchess of . . . .

2 The Peerage

A Duke

Beginning
Formal: My Lord Duke
Social: Dear Duke
*Ending**
Formal: Yours faithfully
Social: Yours sincerely
Envelope
Formal: His Grace the Duke of Battersea
Social: The Duke of Battersea

The Wife of a Duke

Beginning
Formal: Dear Madam
Social: Dear Duchess
Envelope
Formal: Her Grace the Duchess of Battersea
Social: The Duchess of Battersea

The Widow of a Duke†

Beginning and Ending
As for the wife of a Duke.
Envelope
Formal: Her Grace Wendy, Duchess of Battersea
Social: Wendy, Duchess of Battersea

* This ending applies in all instances *except* where otherwise stated.
† *Officially* the widow of a Duke is known as 'The Dowager Duchess of Battersea'. In practice most prefer to use their Christian name: 'Wendy, Duchess of Battersea'. An announcement to this effect is usually made in the Press. The former wife of a Duke continues to use her title, preceded by her Christian name, but is not entitled to the prefix of 'Her Grace'.

A Peer Other than a Duke

(Marquess*, Earl, Viscount, Baron)

Beginning
Formal: My Lord
Social: Dear Lord Putney
Envelope
Formal: The Most Hon. The Marquess of Putney
          The Rt Hon. The Earl of Balham
          The Rt Hon. The Viscount Lambeth
          The Rt Hon. The Lord Wandsworth
Social: The Marquess of Putney
          The Earl of Balham
          The Viscount Lambeth
          The Lord Wandsworth

A Peeress in her Own Right†

Beginning
Formal: Dear Madam
Social: Dear Lady (Baroness) Henfield
Envelope
Formal: The Rt Hon. the Lady (Baroness) Henfield
Social: The Lady (Baroness) Henfield

The Wife of a Peer, Other than a Duke

The wife of a Marquess is a Marchioness
The wife of an Earl is a Countess
The wife of a Viscount is a Viscountess
The wife of a Baron is a Baroness

* 'Marquess' is the spelling adopted in The Role of the House of Lords. 'Marquis' is the French spelling.

† Some peeresses style themselves 'Baroness'. It is a matter of personal choice whether the lady concerned prefers to be addressed as 'Baroness' or 'Lady'.

Beginning
Formal: Dear Madam
Social: Dear Lady Fulham (irrespective of which of the four grades of
peerage is applicable)
Envelope
Formal: The Most Hon. the Marchioness of Putney
             The Rt Hon. the Countess of Balham
             The Rt Hon. the Viscountess Lambeth
             The Rt Hon. the Lady Wandsworth
Social: The Marchioness of Putney
             The Countess of Balham
             The Viscountess Lambeth
             The Lady Wandsworth

The Widow of a Peer, Other than a Duke

Beginning and Ending
As for Peeresses
Envelope
Formal: The Most Hon. Paula, Marchioness of Putney
             The Rt Hon. Beryl, Countess of Balham
             The Rt Hon. Lavender, Viscountess Lambeth
             The Rt Hon. Wanda, Lady Wandsworth
Social: Paula, Marchioness of Putney
             Beryl, Countess of Balham
             Lavender, Viscountess Lambeth
             Wanda, Lady Wandsworth

The Children of a Peer

The son and heir apparent of a Duke, Marquess or Earl may use one
of his father's courtesy titles.

The bearer of a courtesy title is addressed as such a peer with the
following exceptions:

1   A Marquess by Courtesy is not given the formal style of 'The Most
        Hon.'.

2 An Earl, Viscount or Baron by Courtesy is not given the formal style of 'The Right Hon.'.

3 A peer by Courtesy is not addressed as 'The' in correspondence.

The younger sons of a Duke or Marquess have the courtesy style of 'Lord' before Christian name and surname.

The younger sons of an Earl and *all* sons of a Viscount or Baron have the courtesy style of 'The Hon.'* before Christian name and surname.

The daughters of a Duke, Marquess or Earl have the courtesy style of 'The Lady' before Christian name and surname.

The daughters of a Viscount or Baron have the courtesy style of 'The 'Hon.' before Christian name and surname.

The Younger Sons of a Duke or Marquess

Beginning
Formal: My Lord
Social: Dear Lord James
Envelope
Formal and Social: Lord James FitzClarence

The Wife of the Younger Son of a Duke or Marquess

Beginning
Formal: Dear Madam
Social: Dear Lady James
Envelope
Lady James FitzClarence

The Younger Son of an Earl or the Sons of a Viscount or Baron

Beginning
Formal: Dear Sir,
Social: Dear Mr Dutton
Envelope
The Hon. Hubert Dutton

* The abbreviation 'The Honble' is old-fashioned and pedantic, and should be avoided.

The Wife of a Younger Son of an Earl, or of the Son of a Viscount or Baron

The wife of a gentleman with the courtesy style of 'The Honourable' is known by her husband's Christian name and surname, with the addition of 'Mrs' as a prefix. Thus the wife of 'The Hon. Hubert Dutton' is 'The Hon. Mrs Hubert Dutton'.

If she is the daughter of a Duke, Marquess or Earl she will use the style: The Lady Rose Dutton.

If she is the daughter of a Viscount or Baron she is known as 'The Hon. Mrs Dutton'.

'The Honourable' is *never* used in conversation, on invitations or on visiting cards.

Beginning
Formal: Dear Madam
Social: Dear Mrs Dutton
Envelope
Formal and Social: The Hon. Mrs Hubert Dutton

The Daughter of a Duke, Marquess or Earl

Beginning
Formal: Dear Madam
Social: Dear Lady Deborah
Envelope
Formal and Social: The Lady Deborah Clarke

The Daughter of a Viscount or Baron

Beginning
Formal: Dear Madam
Social: Dear Miss (Mrs) Lee
Envelope
Formal and Social: The Hon. Ann Lee (if unmarried)
                              The Hon. Mrs Lee

3 Other Titles and Styles

A Baronet

Beginning
Formal: Dear Sir
Social: Dear Sir Nicholas
Envelope
Formal and Social: Sir Nicholas Samuelson, Bt*

The Wife of a Baronet

Beginning
Formal: Dear Madam
Social: Dear Lady Samuelson
Envelope
Formal and Social: Lady Samuelson

A Knight

Beginning
Formal: Dear Sir
Social: Dear Sir Philip
Envelope
Formal and Social: Sir Philip O'Brien (with the appropriate letters after
                    his name)

The Wife of a Knight

Beginning
Formal: Dear Madam
Social: Dear Lady O'Brien
Envelope
Formal and Social: Lady O'Brien

* Bt is now more commonly used than the more old-fashioned Bart, but either is correct.
When a baronet is a Member of Parliament the letters MP follow the title both officially
and socially: Sir Nicholas Samuelson Bt, MP.

A Dame

Beginning
Formal: Dear Madam
Social: Dear Dame Ruth
Envelope
Formal and Social: Dame Ruth Lister DBE (or applicable order)*

Untitled Gentleman

It is for the writer to decide whether to address his correspondent as Mr Herbert Rees or Herbert Rees Esq. The latter style is now customary in most walks of life in Great Britain and Ireland and in many of those English-speaking countries which formerly constituted the British Empire. In the United States, Canada, Australia and New Zealand, however, the style of Mr is generally used. Herbert Rees is considered impolite, except for schoolboys. The style of Master Herbert Rees has largely gone out of fashion and is generally unpopular with boys.
Beginning
Formal: Dear Sir
          Dear Mr Rees
Social:
Envelope
Formal and Social: Herbert Rees Esq. is preferred (see above).

Untitled Married Lady

If the Christian name of the lady's husband is unknown, it is more usual to address her as Mrs Rees than Mrs Louella Rees.

It is incorrect for a widow to be addressed by her own Christian names or initials, as this implies that her marriage was dissolved.
Beginning
Formal: Dear Madam
Social: Dear Mrs Rees
Envelope
  1 Wife or widow of the head of the family: Mrs Rees
  2 Wives or widows of other members of the family: Mrs Herbert Rees
  3 Divorced ladies: Mrs Louella Rees *or* Mrs L. A. Rees

* A peeress or holder of a courtesy title who is appointed a dame adds the appropriate letters after her name: The Countess of Berkhamsted, DCVO; Lady Rachel Bissell, DBE.

Untitled Unmarried Lady

Beginning
Formal: Dear Madam
Social: Dear Miss Jackson
Envelope
Eldest unmarried daughter: Miss Jackson
Otherwise: Miss Morwenna Jackson

4 The Clergy

Anglican

The Archbishops of Canterbury and York

Beginning
Formal: My Lord Archbishop *or* Your Grace
Social: Dear Archbishop
Ending
Formal: I have the honour to remain, my Lord Archbishop, Your Grace's devoted and obedient servant.
Social: Yours sincerely
Envelope
The Most Reverend* and Right Hon. the Lord Archbishop of Canterbury/York

A Bishop

Beginning
Formal: My Lord Bishop
Social: Dear Bishop
Ending
Formal: I have the honour to remain Your Lordship's obedient servant
Social: Yours sincerely

* The Reverend may in all instances be abbreviated to 'The Rev.'.

Envelope
The Right Reverend the Lord Bishop of Barchester*

It is a matter of debate whether a Suffragan Bishop is entitled to the style of 'Lord' Bishop, but the prefix is customarily accorded as a matter of courtesy. However, he is not so styled in official documents.

Since the Episcopal Church is not the State Church of Scotland, a Bishop has no official recognition. He is therefore addressed as 'The Right Rev. Donald McTavish, Bishop of Corstorphine'.

Overseas Bishops are styled as Bishops of the Church of England with these exceptions:

The Most Reverend the Bishop of Meath

The Metropolitan of the Church of India, Pakistan, Burma and Sri Lanka has the following style:

The Most Reverend the Bishop of Calcutta (or appropriate See)

The Bishop *on* the Niger Delta

The Bishop *in* Egypt

The Bishop *in* Iran

A Dean

Beginning
Formal: Very Reverend Sir
Social: Dear Dean
Envelope
The Very Reverend the Dean of Grantchester

An Archdeacon

Beginning
Formal: Venerable Sir
Social: Dear Archdeacon
Envelope
The Venerable the Archdeacon of Mellstock

A Canon

Beginning
Formal and Social: Dear Canon *or* Dear Canon Lawson

* The Bishop of London is always a Privy Counsellor and is accordingly addressed as 'Right Reverend and Right Honourable'.

A Rector, Vicar* or Assistant Curate

Beginning
Formal and Social: Dear Mr Gray *or* Dear Vicar
Envelope
The Reverend John Gray
The form 'The Reverend Gray' or 'Reverend Gray' is incorrect and should never be used.

If a clergyman succeeds to a title or has a courtesy title or style, the ecclesiastical style precedes the temporal:

The Reverend the Viscount Parsons
The Venerable the Hon. Hugh Pugh
The Reverend Sir Oliver Sloane, Bt

Roman Catholic

The Pope

Beginning
Your Holiness or Most Holy Father
Ending
For Roman Catholics: I have the honour to be Your Holiness's most humble child

For non-Roman Catholics: I have the honour to be Your Holiness's most obedient servant
Envelope
His Holiness The Pope

A Cardinal

Beginning
Formal: Your Eminence *or* My Lord Cardinal
Social: Dear Cardinal Elliot

---

* The difference between a Rector and a Vicar is now purely nominal. In former times a Rector had the parsonage and was in receipt of the greater tithes. The Vicar was in receipt of the lesser tithes only.

Ending
Formal: I have the honour to remain Your Eminence's devoted and obedient child*
Social: Yours sincerely
Envelope
If an Archbishop: His Eminence the Cardinal Archbishop of Westminster
If not an Archbishop: His Eminence Cardinal Elliot

An Archbishop

Beginning
Formal: My Lord Archbishop
Social: Dear Archbishop
Ending
Formal: I remain, Your Grace, Yours faithfully
Social: Yours sincerely
Envelope
His Grace the Archbishop of Appolonia

A Bishop

Beginning
Formal: My Lord *or* My Lord Bishop
Social: Dear Bishop *or* Dear Bishop Bartlett
Ending
Formal: I remain, My Lord, Yours faithfully
Social: Yours sincerely
Envelope
His Lordship the Bishop of Transylvania *or* The Right Reverend Robert
Bartlett, Bishop of Transylvania

A Priest

Beginning
Formal: Dear Reverend Father
Social: Dear Father Peter or Dear Father Hunt
Envelope
The Reverend Peter Hunt

* Roman Catholics in Holy Orders write servant instead of child.

5   The Royal Navy

An Admiral of the Fleet

Beginning
Formal: If a Peer – My Lord
          Otherwise – Dear Sir
Social: Dear Lord Flamborough *or*
          Dear Sir William
Envelope
Admiral of the Fleet the Lord Flamborough, GCB, KBE, *or*
Admiral of the Fleet Sir William Targett, GCB, KBE, DSO

An Admiral, Vice-Admiral, Rear-Admiral

All three ranks are known socially as Admiral. The letters RN (Royal Navy) do *not* appear after their orders and decorations.

Beginning
Formal: Dear Sir
Social: Dear Sir Horatio (if a Knight)
          Dear Admiral Nelson
Envelope
*Admiral Sir James White, GCE, KCB
*Vice-Admiral Sir Henry Green, KBE, DSC
*Rear-Admiral Evan Harrington, CB, OBE

A Captain, Commander or Lieutenant

Beginning
Formal: Dear Sir
Social: *Dear Captain Jones
          *Dear Commander Smith
          *Dear Lieutenant Robinson
Envelope
*Captain David Jones, CBE, RN
*Commander Simon Smith, OBE, RN
*Lieutenant Robinson

  * When writing socially, orders of merit or of knighthood are customarily omitted, with the exception of the KBE.

A Sub-Lieutenant

Beginning
Formal: Dear Sir
Social: Dear Mr Dexter
Envelope
*Sub-Lieutenant Harold Dexter, RN

6   The Army

A Field-Marshal

Beginning
Formal: If a Peer – My Lord
            Otherwise – Dear Sir
Social: Dear Lord Norris *or*
            Dear Sir George *or*
            Dear Field-Marshal
Envelope
*Field-Marshal the Lord Norris, GCB, GBE, DSO *or*
*Field-Marshal Sir George Gordon, GCB, KBE, DSO

A General, Lieutenant-General, Major-General

All three ranks are known socially as General.
Beginning
Formal: Dear Sir
Social: Dear Sir Daniel *or*
            Dear General Jilks *or*
            Dear General
Envelope
*General Sir Daniel Jilks, GCB, DSO, ADC
*Lieutenant-General Sir Charles Garth, DBE, CB
*Major-General Oliver Grant, CBE, DSO, MC

* These ranks should not be abbreviated.

215

A Brigadier, Colonel, Lieutenant-Colonel, Major or Captain

Colonels and Lieutenant-Colonels are both referred to as Colonel, except on the envelope.

Beginning
Formal: Dear Sir
Social: Dear Brigadier Fairway *or*
Dear Brigadier
(Dear Colonel and Dear Major are acceptable, *not* Dear Captain.)

Envelope
The Regiment or Corps (or abbreviations) may be added below the name of an officer on the active list.

   *Lieutenant-Colonel Robert Hillyard, DSO,
     Grenadier Guards
   Major Charles Porter, MC,
     KOYLI

A Lieutenant or Second Lieutenant

Beginning
Formal: Dear Sir
Social: Dear Mr Bennett
Envelope
Adam Bennett Esq.,
   The Royal Hussars

---

* This rank should not be abbreviated.

7 The Royal Air Force

Marshal of the Royal Air Force

As for Admiral of the Fleet.

Air Chief Marshal, Air Marshal or Air Vice-Marshal

All three ranks are known socially as Air Marshal. The letters RAF may
follow the name.
Beginning
Formal: Dear Sir
Social: Dear Sir Roy *or*
          Dear Air Marshal Macdonald
Envelope
Air Chief Marshal Sir Arthur Cooper, GCB, CBE, DFC, RAF
Air Marshal Sir Newman Waters, KCB, CBE, DFC, RAF
Air Vice-Marshal John Rodgers, CB, AFC, RAF

Air Commodore, Group Captain, Wing Commander, Squadron Leader or Flight Lieutenant

Beginning
Formal: Dear Sir
Social: Dear Air Commodore Gilbert
          Dear Group Captain Hubbard
          etc.
Envelope
Air Commodore Mark Gilbert, DFC, RAF

Flying Officer or Pilot Officer

Beginning
Formal: Dear Sir
Social: Dear Mr Boythorn
Envelope
Lawrence Boythorn Esq., AFC, RAF

8   Members of Her Majesty's Government

Beginning
Formal: Dear Sir/Madam
Social: Dear Mr Gowan

If the writer knows the Minister personally and the subject of his letter concerns his Department, it is permissible to write to him by his appointment:

Dear Prime Minister
Dear Lord Chancellor
Dear Chancellor (of the Exchequer)
Dear Lord President (of the Council)
Dear Home/Foreign Secretary *or* Dear Secretary of State
Dear Solicitor-General
Dear Attorney-General
Dear Lord Advocate
Dear Minister etc.

Envelope
Formal: The Secretary of State for Foreign Affairs
Social: The Rt Hon. Sir Thomas Field KBE, MP, Secretary of State for Foreign Affairs

9   The Legal Profession

The Lord Chancellor

Beginning
Formal: My Lord
Social: Dear Lord Chancellor
Envelope
The Rt Hon. The Lord Chancellor

The Lord Chief Justice

Beginning
Formal: My Lord
Social: Dear Lord Chief Justice
Envelope
The Rt Hon. the Lord Chief Justice of England

The Master of the Rolls

Beginning
Formal: Sir
Social: Dear Master of the Rolls
Envelope
The Rt Hon. The Master of the Rolls

A Lord Justice of the Court of Appeal

Beginning
Formal: My Lord
Social: Dear Lord Justice
Envelope
The Rt Hon. the Lord Justice Lambourne

A Judge of High Court

Beginning
Formal: Dear Sir
On Judicial Matters: My Lord
Social: Dear Judge (excluding the surname)
Envelope
Formal and Judicial: The Hon. Mr Justice Huddlestone
Social: Sir Bernard Huddlestone

A Judge of County Court

Beginning
Formal and Judicial: Dear Sir
Social: Dear Judge
Envelope
Formal and Social: His Honour Judge Featherstone

If a Knight:
Formal: His Honour Judge Featherstone
Social: Sir Solomon Featherstone

A Recorder

Beginning
Formal: Dear Sir
Official: Dear Mr Recorder
Social: Dear Mr Claypole
Envelope
Formal and Social: Norman Claypole Esq.,
Official: Norman Claypole Esq., QC, Recorder of Bolterton

A Queen's Counsel

When a Barrister becomes a Queen's Counsel the letters QC are placed after the name. This includes County Court Judges but excludes High Court Judges and higher legal appointments.

10   The Medical Profession

A Doctor of Medicine

Beginning
Formal: Dear Sir
Social: Dear Dr Denny
Envelope
Dr Philip Denny, MD, FRCP

Those with doctorates, masterships and fellowships should be addressed on the envelope with the appropriate letters. Others who practise medicine (MRCS, LRCP, MB, BS, BM, B Chir, etc.) may be addressed on the envelope as Dr Frederick Hamson if the exact qualifying diplomas are not known.

A Surgeon or Gynaecologist

Beginning
Formal: Dear Sir
Social: Dear Mr Endicott
Envelopes
George Endicott Esq., MS, FRCS
William Ferraby Esq., FRCOG

11   Diplomatic Appointments

A Foreign Ambassador Accredited to the United Kingdom and a
   Commonwealth High Commissioner

Beginning
Formal: Your Excellency*
Social: Dear Ambassador
              Dear High Commissioner
Ending
Formal: I have the honour to be, with the highest consideration, Your
   Excellency's obedient servant
Social: Believe me,
              My Dear Ambassador/High Commissioner,
              Yours very sincerely
Envelope
Formal: His Excellency the Transylvanian Ambassador†
Social: His Excellency Herr Manfred Franks

A British Ambassador Accredited to a Foreign Country

Beginning
Formal: Sir
Social: Dear Ambassador

---

* An Ambassador's wife is *not* styled Her Excellency, and is addressed and referred to by
her name.

† His Excellency precedes all other styles, titles or ranks except *Royal* or *Serene Highness*.
Service ranks immediately follow it: His Excellency General Count Feliciani.

221

Ending
Formal: I have the honour to be,
       Sir,
       Your Excellency's Obedient Servant
Social: Believe me,
       My dear Ambassador,
       Yours very sincerely
Envelope
Peer: His Excellency the Lord Grandison, KCMG
Privy Councillor: His Excellency the Rt Hon. Simon Lee, CMG
Knight: His Excellency Sir Charles Mirabel
Esquire: His Excellency Mr George Sampson CMG ('Esq.' is not used
  with His Excellency)

A Consul-General, Consul or Vice-Consul

A Consul-General, Consul or Vice-Consul who holds Her Majesty's
commission is entitled to the letters 'HM' before the appointment. The
style 'HBM' (Her Britannic Majesty) is no longer used.
Beginning
Formal: Dear Sir
Social: Dear Mr Holt
Envelope
Francis Holt Esq., CMG,
HM Consul-General,
British Consulate General

A Governor-General, Governor or Lieutenant-Governor

Beginning
Formal: My Lord (if a peer)
       Sir
Social: Dear Lord Hazlewood
       Dear Sir Guy
       Dear Mr Hazlewood
Ending
Formal: I have the honour to be,
       My Lord (Sir),
       Your Excellency's obedient servant,

Social: Yours sincerely
Envelope
His Excellency* The Lord Hazlewood, KCB, Governor-General of Saturnalia
His Excellency Sir Guy Hazlewood, KCB, Governor of Bandola
His Excellency Mr Guy Hazlewood, CMG, Governor of St Philomena

12   Civic Appointments

A Lord Mayor

The Lord Mayors of London and York are styled 'The Right Honourable'. Other Lord Mayors are so styled only when the Queen grants them the privilege. These are the Lord Mayors of Cardiff, Belfast and the state capitals of Australia. Lord Mayors of other cities are styled 'The Right Worshipful.'†

Beginning
Formal: My Lord Mayor
Social: Dear Lord Mayor
Envelope
The Right Honourable the Lord Mayor of Cardiff
The Right Worshipful the Lord Mayor of Coventry

A Mayor of a City or Borough

Beginning
Formal: Mr Mayor‡
Social: Dear Mr Mayor
Envelope
City: The Right Worshipful the Mayor of Bath
Borough: The Worshipful the Mayor of Southwark

* The wife of a Governor-General but *not* of a Governor is accorded the style of 'Her Excellency' within the country administered by her husband.
† A Lady Mayoress is not accorded the style of 'The Right Honourable' or 'The Right Worshipful'.
‡ This applies even though the Mayor be a peer of the realm or a lady.

Foreign Phrases and their Meanings

ab initio (L.), from the beginning

à compte (Fr.), on account, in part payment

ad hoc (L.), for this [particular occasion]

ad infinitum (L.), without end

ad nauseam (L.), to a sickening degree

ad valorem (L.), according to value

affaire d'honneur (Fr.), a duel

a fortiori (L.), with better reason

aide-memoire (Fr.), an aid to memory

à la mode (Fr.), according to fashion

Alma Mater (L.), literally benign mother; used of one's university

alter ego (L.), one's second self

amour propre (Fr.), self-love, vanity

annus mirabilis (L.), the year of wonders

ante (L.), before

à outrance (Fr.), to the bitter end

a priori (L.), by deduction

à propos (Fr.), to the point

au contraire (Fr.), on the contrary

au courant (Fr.), well acquainted with

au fait (Fr.), well instructed in

au fond (Fr.), at the bottom - of the question or problem - not the sea or garden

au revoir (Fr.), goodbye; until we meet again

avant-garde (Fr.), the advanced guard - usually of fashion

à volonté (Fr.), at will

à votre santé (Fr.), to your health

bête noire (Fr.), literally black beast; one's pet aversion

blasé (Fr.), bored, sick of pleasure

bona fide (L.), in good faith, genuinely

bonhomie (Fr.), good nature

bonne bouche (Fr.), a titbit

bon ton (Fr.), good taste

bon voyage (Fr.), [have a] good journey

carte blanche (Fr.), unlimited power to act

causus belli (L.), cause of war

chacun à son goût (Fr.), to each according to his taste

chargé d'affaires (Fr.), an official who acts as deputy to an ambassador

chef-d'œuvre (Fr.), a masterpiece

ci-devant (Fr.), former

comme il faut (Fr.), as it should be

compos mentis (L.), in one's right mind

compte rendu (Fr.), account rendered

con amore (It.), with love

contretemps (Fr.), a setback

coup de grâce (Fr.), the finishing stroke

coup d'état (Fr.), a change of government by sudden and violent means

coup de théâtre (Fr.), a sudden, sensational act

crème de la crème (Fr.), literally cream of the cream; the very best

cui bono? (L.), who gains by it? (usually by the crime in a lawsuit)

début (Fr.), a first appearance

de facto (L.), actually, in fact. (opposite of *de jure*)

Dei gratia (L.), by the grace of God

de jure (L.), according to law, by right

de novo (L.), anew

de profundis (L.), from the depths

dernier cri (Fr.), the latest thing (in fashion)

de trop (Fr.), too much, not wanted, in the way

dies irae (L.), the day of wrath

dies non (L.), a day when judges do not sit

double entendre (Fr.), double meaning. (The correct form is *entente* but *entendre* is more commonly used.)

dramatis personae (L.), the characters in a play

Ecce Homo! (L.), 'Behold the Man' (John xix, 5)

embarras de richesse (Fr.), a superabundance of wealth

en bloc (Fr.), in a lump, in bulk

encore (Fr.), again, once more

en famille (Fr.), with one's own family

en fête (Fr.), on holiday; in festive mood

en masse (Fr.), in a body, all together

en passant (Fr.), in passing, by the way

en route (Fr.), on the way, bound for

entre nous (Fr.), between ourselves

esprit de corps (Fr.), team spirit

etiquette (Fr.), the rules of behaviour in polite society

ex cathedra (L.), with authority

ex officio (L.), by virtue of one's office

ex parte (L.), on one side, partisan

fait accompli (Fr.), an accomplished fact, a thing already done and not now worth worrying about

faux pas (Fr.), a false step, a blunder – usually of a social nature

felo de se (L.), literally felon of himself; suicide

femme de chambre (Fr.), a chambermaid

Fidei defensor (L.), Defender of the Faith – title granted to Henry VIII by Pope Leo X

gloria in excelsis Deo (L.), glory to God in the highest

gratis (L.), free

habitué (Fr.), a frequenter, a regular customer

hic jacet (L.), here lies

honi soit qui mal y pense (Fr.), shame be to him who thinks evil (motto of the Order of the Garter)

hors de combat (Fr.), out of the fight, disabled

hôtel de ville (Fr.), a town hall

idée fixe (Fr.), a fixed idea, one that no persuasion can alter

impasse (Fr.), a deadlock

in camera (L.), [of legal proceedings] heard in private, not in open court

in extremis (L.), at the point of death

in loco parentis (L.), in place of one's parents

in memoriam (L.), in memory of

in situ (L.), in position

inter alia (L.), among other things

inter nos (L.), between ourselves

in toto (L.), entirely

ipsissima verba (L.), the very words

ipso facto (L.), by the fact itself

je ne sais quoi (Fr.), I know not what

jeu d'esprit (Fr.), a witticism

joie de vivre (Fr.), joy of life, high spirits

juste milieu (Fr.), the golden mean

labor omnia vincit (L.), work overcomes all [problems]

laissez-faire (Fr.), leave alone – the principle of non-interference, especially by a government in commercial matters

lapsus linguae (L.), a slip of the tongue

lares et penates (L.), household gods

laus Deo (L.), praise [be] to God

lèse-majesté (Fr.), high treason

Lingua Franca (It.), the mixed language spoken by Europeans in the East; any similar jargon

lite pendente (L.), during the trial

locum tenens (L.), a deputy or substitute, usually abbreviated to locum

ma chère (f.), *mon cher* (m.) (Fr.), my dear

ma foi! (Fr.), upon my word!

magnum opus (L.), an author's chief work

maître d'hôtel (Fr.), head waiter

malaise (Fr.), discomfiture, uneasiness

mal de mer (Fr.), sea-sickness

mariage de convenance (Fr.), a marriage of convenience

mea culpa (L.), my own fault

memento mori (L.), remember that you must die

mésalliance (Fr.), marriage with a social inferior

mise en scène (Fr.), the scenery and setting of a play; figuratively, the setting of any event

modus operandi (L.), way of working

more suo (L.), in his own way

multum in parvo (L.), much in little

née (Fr.), born (used before a married woman's maiden name)

nem. con. (L.), no one contradicting (a contraction of *nemine contradicente*; the extended form is rarely used)

nil desperandum (L.), despair of nothing, *not* never despair

n'importe! (Fr.), never mind!

noblesse oblige (Fr.), rank has its obligations

nom de plume (Fr.), a pen name

non sequitur (abbr. *non. seq.*) (L.), it does not follow logically

nota bene (abbr. *NB*) (L.), mark well

nulli secundus (L.), second to none

obit (L.), he/she died

obiter dictum (L.), a thing said in passing

oeuvres (Fr.), works

on dit (Fr.), literally one says; gossip, rumour

opus (L.), a work, pl. *opera*

par excellence (Fr.), pre-eminently

pari passu (L.), at the same rate

parole d'honneur (Fr.), word of honour

pâté de foie gras (Fr.), goose-liver pâté

Pater noster (L.), Our Father; hence *paternoster*, the Lord's Prayer

pension (Fr.), a boarding house

per annum (L.), yearly

per aspera ad astra (L.), through adversity to the stars

per centum (abbr. *per cent*, %) (L.), for, in or to every hundred

per contra (L.), on the other hand

per diem (L.), by the day

per se (L.), by himself, herself, itself, themselves

persona [non] grata (L.), an [un-] acceptable person

pied-à-terre (Fr.), temporary lodgings

pis aller (Fr.), last resource, makeshift

post (L.), after

post mortem (L.), after death. A post-mortem examination of a body is made to determine the cause of death

poste restante (Fr.), (of letters, etc.) to remain until called for

prima facie (L.), first impression; at first sight

pro bono publico (L.), for the public good

pro forma (L.), as a matter of form

pro rata (L.), in proportion

quid pro quo (L.), one thing for another

qui vive? (Fr.), literally who lives?; to be on the *qui vive* is to be on the alert

raison d'être (Fr.), the purpose of existence

rapport (Fr.), affinity, harmony

reductio ad absurdum (L.), an obviously absurd conclusion

res judicata (L.), a thing already decided

résumé (Fr.), a concise summary

resurgam (L.), I will rise again

sang-froid (Fr.), literally cold blood: calmness, indifference

sans doute (Fr.), without doubt

sans peur et sans reproche (Fr.), fearless and blameless – sobriquet applied to the chevalier Bayard (1476–1524)

sans souci (Fr.), without a care

sauve qui peut (Fr.), let him save himself who can

savoir faire (Fr.), tact

semper fidelis (L.), always faithful

semper idem (L.), always the same

sic (L.), thus (often used to call attention to a quoted me*s*take [*sic*])

226

s'il vous plâit (Fr.), if you please

sine die (L.), [postponed] without a day [being appointed]

sine qua non (L.), an indispensable condition

status quo (L.), the same state as before

Sturm and Drang (Ger.), storm and stress

sub judice (L.), under consideration

sub rosa (L.), literally under the rose; privately

sui generis (L.), of his, her, its, their own kind

suppressio veri (L.), suppression of the truth

tableau vivant (Fr.), literally living picture; a scene in which statues or pictures are represented by living people

table d'hôte (Fr.), a set menu, the opposite of *à la carte*

tant mieux (Fr.), so much the better

tant pis (Fr.) so much the worse

tempus fugit (L.), time flies

tête-à-tête (Fr.), a private interview or conversation

tour de force (Fr.), a feat of strength or skill

tout ensemble (Fr.), the general effect

verbatim (L.), word for word

via media (L.), a middle course

vice versa (L.), conversely, the other way round

vis-à-vis (Fr.), facing, opposite; relative to

viva voce (L.), literally by the living voice; oral, orally

vive le roi (la reine)! (Fr.), long live the King (Queen)!

vox populi (L.), the voice of the people

227

Abbreviations in Common Use

A1	indicates a ship in the first class at Lloyd's	Ltd	Limited
a/c	account	m	metre
ad lib	at pleasure	M	in Roman numerals, 1000
AD	in the year of our Lord		
a.m.	before midday (*ante meridiem*)	mm	millimetre
		MP	Member of Parliament, or Military Police
BC	Before Christ		
°C	degrees Celsius, Centigrade	MS	manuscript
		MSS	manuscripts
Cantab.	Cambridge	NB	note or mark well
cm	centimetre	NS	New Style
Co.	Company	o/a	on account of
COD	cash on delivery	ob.	*obiit*, died
cr.	credit or creditor	op	out of print
cwt	a hundredweight or 112 lb	OS	Old Style or Outsize
		o/s	out of stock
		Oxon.	Oxford
D	in Roman numerals, 500	oz	ounce
do	*ditto* (Ital.) the same	p.m.	after midday (*post meridiem*)
Dr	Doctor or debtor		
dsp	died without issue	PO	Post Office
DV	God willing	po	postal order
eg	for example	pp or per pro	for and on behalf of
etc.	(*et cetera*) and the rest		
°F	degrees Fahrenheit	ppa	per power of attorney
fob	freight on board	ppc	(*pour prendre congé*) to take leave
g	gram		
gr	grain	PS	postscript
id or *idem*	the same	PTO	please turn over
ie	that is	QED	Which was to be proved (*Quod erat demonstrandum*)
IHS	Jesus the Saviour of Men (*Hominum Salvator*)		
		qv	which see
		Rev.	Reverend
ILO	International Labour Office	RSVP	(*Répondez, s'il vous plaît*) Reply if you please.
INRI	Jesus of Nazareth, King of the Jews		
		Rt Hon.	Right Honourable
kg	kilogram	*sic*	thus
km	kilometre	St	Saint or Street
l	litre	V	in Roman numerals, 5
L	in Roman numerals, 50	VAT	Value added tax
£	a pound sterling	viz	namely
lb	a pound weight	X	in Roman numerals, 10

Abbreviations of Titles Which Are in Common Use

AACCA	Associate of the Association of Certified and Corporate Accountants
AAI	Associate of the Chartered Auctioneers' and Estate Agents' Institute
ACA	Associate of the Institute of Chartered Accountants
ACCA	Associate of the Association of Certified Accountants
ACCS	Associate of the Corporation of Secretaries
ACGI	Associate of the City and Guilds of London Institute
ACIS	Associate of the Institute of Chartered Secretaries and Administrators
AFC	Air Force Cross
AFM	Air Force Medal
AMICE	Associate Member of the Institution of Civil Engineers
AMI MechE	Associate Member of the Institution of Mechanical Engineers
ARA	Associate Member of the Royal Academy
ARCM	Associate of the Royal College of Music
ARIBA	Associate Member of the Institute of British Architects

ARICS	Associate Member of the Institute of Chartered Surveyors
BA	Bachelor of Arts
Bart	Baronet
BCL	Bachelor of Civil Law
BD	Bachelor of Divinity
BEM	British Empire Medal
BEng	Bachelor of Engineering
BL	Bachelor of Law
BLit(t)	Bachelor of Literature *or* Letters
BM	Bachelor of Medicine
BMus	Bachelor of Music
BS	Bachelor of Surgery
Bt	Baronet
CB	Companion of the Order of the Bath
CBE	Commander of the Order of the British Empire
CE	Civil Engineer
CGM	Conspicuous Gallantry Medal
CH	Companion of Honour
ChB	Bachelor of Surgery
ChM	Master of Surgery
CIE	Companion of the Order of the Indian Empire
CMG	Companion of the Order of St Michael and St George
CVO	Commander of the Royal Victorian Order

DBE	Dame Commander of the Order of the British Empire	FZS	Fellow of the Zoological Association
D Ch	Doctor of Surgery	GBE	Knight or Dame Grand Cross of the Order of the British Empire
DCL	Doctor of Civil Law		
DCM	Distinguished Conduct Medal		
		GC	George Cross
DD	Doctor of Divinity	GCB	Knight Grand Cross of the Order of the Bath
DFC	Distinguished Flying Cross		
		GCIE	Knight Grand Commander of the Order of the Indian Empire
DFM	Distinguished Flying Medal		
DL	Deputy-Lieutenant	GCMG	Knight Grand Cross of the Order of St Michael and St George
DLit *or* Litt	Doctor of Literature *or* Letters		
DPh or DPhil	Doctor of Philosophy		
		GCSI	Knight Grand Commander of the Order of the Star of India
DSC	Distinguished Service Cross		
D Sc	Doctor of Science	GCVO	Knight Grand Cross of the Royal Victorian Order
DSM	Distinguished Service Medal		
DSO	Distinguished Service Order	GM	George Medal
		ISO	Imperial Service Order
FCA	Fellow of the Institute of Chartered Accountants		
		JP	Justice of the Peace
FGS	Fellow of the Geological Society	KBE	Knight Commander of the Order of the British Empire
FRCM	Fellow of the Royal College of Music		
FRCOG	Fellow of the Royal College of Gynaecologists	KC	King's Counsel
		KCB	Knight Commander of the Order of the Bath
FRCP	Fellow of the Royal College of Physicians		
FRCS	Fellow of the Royal College of Surgeons	KCIE	Knight Commander of the Order of the Indian Empire
FRGS	Fellow of the Royal Geographical Society		
		KCMG	Knight Commander of St Michael and St George
FRHS	Fellow of the Royal Horticultural Society		
FRIBA	Fellow of the Institute of British Architects	KCVO	Knight Commander of the Royal Victorian Order
FRS	Fellow of the Royal Society		
		KG	Knight Commander of the Order of the Garter
FRSA	Fellow of the Royal Society of Arts		
FSA	Fellow of the Society of Antiquaries	KP	Knight Commander of the Order of St Patrick

KT	Knight Commander of the Order of the Thistle	MRCP	Member of the Royal College of Physicians
		MRCS	Member of the Royal College of Surgeons
Lit D *or* Litt D	Doctor of Literature *or* Letters	MRI	Member of the Royal Institution
LLB	Bachelor of Laws	MS	Mastery of Surgery
LLD	Doctor of Laws	MSc	Master of Science
LRCP	Licentiate of the Royal College of Physicians	MusB	Bachelor of Music
		MusM	Master of Music
LRCS	Licentiate of the Royal College of Surgeons	OBE	Officer of the Order of the British Empire
		OM	Order of Merit
MA	Master of Arts		
MB	Bachelor of Medicine	PC	Privy Councillor
MBE	Member of the Order of the British Empire	PhD	Doctor of Philosophy
MC	Military Cross	QC	Queen's Counsel
MCh	Master of Surgery		
MD	Doctor of Medicine	RA	Royal Academician
MI ChemE	Member of the Institution of Chemical Engineers	RAM	(Member of) The Royal Academy of Music
MIEE	Member of the Institution of Electrical Engineers	SEN	State Enrolled Nurse
		SJ	Society of Jesus (Jesuits)
		SRN	State Registered Nurse
MI MechE	Member of the Institution of Mechanical Engineers	TD	Territorial Efficiency Decoration
MM	Military Medal		
MP	Member of Parliament	VC	Victoria Cross